T4-ABL-029

CHAVEZ HIGH SCHOOL
LIBRARY
HOUSTON, TEXAS

Population

Look for these and other books in the Lucent Overview series:

> Acid Rain
> AIDS
> Animal Rights
> The Beginning of Writing
> Dealing with Death
> Drugs and Sports
> Drug Trafficking
> Endangered Species
> Garbage
> Hazardous Waste
> Homeless Children
> Oil Spills
> The Olympic Games
> Population
> Rainforests
> Smoking
> Soviet-American Relations
> Special Effects in the Movies
> Teen Alcoholism
> The UFO Challenge
> Vietnam

Population

by Don Nardo

LUCENT
B·O·O·K·S

CHAVEZ HIGH SCHOOL
LIBRARY
HOUSTON, TEXAS

LUCENT Overview Series

OUR ENDANGERED PLANET

LUCENT Overview Series OUR ENDANGERED PLANET

Library of Congress Cataloging-in-Publication Data

Nardo, Don, 1947-
    Population / by Don Nardo.
       p. cm. — (Lucent overview series. Our endangered planet)
    Includes bibliographical references and index.
    Summary: Considers the global consequences of continued population growth and the various options for dealing with its impact on the environment and natural resources.
    ISBN 1-56006-123-5
    1. Population—Juvenile literature.   2. Population policy—Juvenile literature.   [1. Population.]   I. Title.   II. Series.
HB883.N37   1991
304.6—dc20   90-23525

No part of this book may be reproduced or used in any form or by any means, electrical, mechanical, or otherwise, including, but not limited to, photocopy, recording, or any information storage and retrieval system, without prior written permission from the publisher.

© Copyright 1991 by Lucent Books, Inc.
P.O. Box 289011, San Diego, CA 92198-0011

Contents

INTRODUCTION	7
CHAPTER ONE A Global Population Problem	11
CHAPTER TWO The Developing Countries	23
CHAPTER THREE The Developed Countries	39
CHAPTER FOUR Dangers to the Environment	51
CHAPTER FIVE Population Strategies and Solutions	71
GLOSSARY	88
SUGGESTIONS FOR FURTHER READING	90
WORKS CONSULTED	91
INDEX	93
ABOUT THE AUTHOR	96
PICTURE CREDITS	96

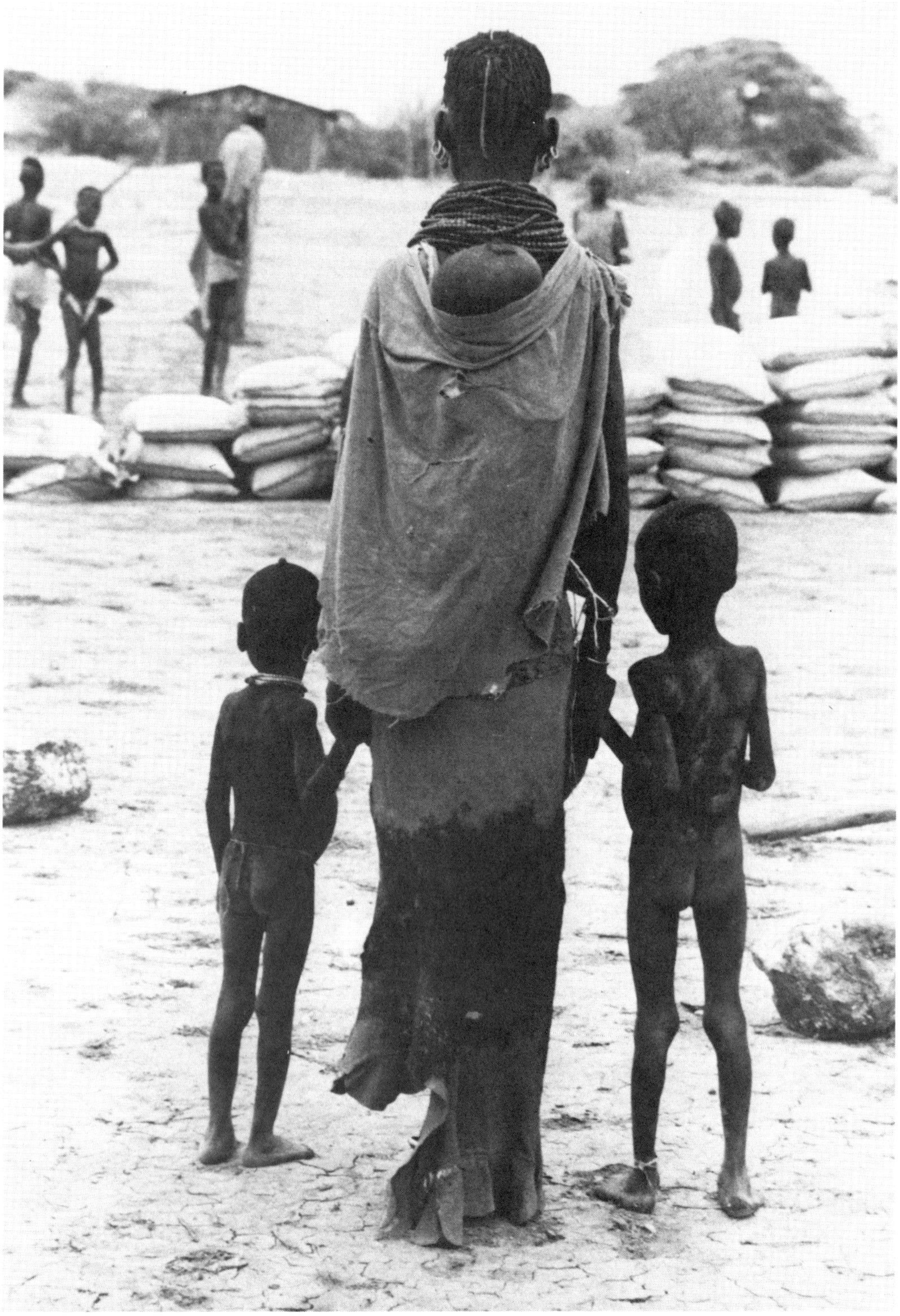

Introduction

THROUGHOUT HISTORY, overpopulation has plagued humanity. When any population becomes too large for the amount of available food and water, people suffer from malnutrition, disease, and, eventually, starvation. One unfortunate event, such as a severe drought, can cause an entire population to endure catastrophic famine, or severe shortage of food.

One such incident, thought by historians to be the worst famine ever to strike a group of people, occurred in China between 1876 and 1879. At the time, China had a population of more than 100 million, the highest in the world. Almost all the Chinese were poor farmers who relied on only one or two crops for food. In this case, the staple crops were grains like wheat and rice. Even in good years, the Chinese farmers produced barely enough grain to feed the country's rapidly growing population. When these crops failed, widespread starvation was the result.

China's disastrous famine struck the country when the crops failed because of drought. Beginning in 1873, the amount of rain decreased each year until 1876, when no rain fell at all and mass starvation began. Hungry people were so desperate, they resorted to robbery and murder to obtain food. Husbands sold their wives into prostitution,

(opposite page) A mother and children wait for food distribution at an emergency station in Ethiopia. The planet's population is approximately 5.3 billion. Access to food, housing, energy, and medical care is not readily available to many of these people.

Tens of thousands of people in the developing countries have died of starvation. Here, tribal Africans wait for food to be distributed.

and parents sold their children to get enough money to buy food.

Everywhere in China people prayed for rain. But in 1877 and 1878 the rain still did not come. Desperate Chinese peasants ate tree bark, grass seeds, and the rotten reeds from the roofs of their cottages. Timothy Richard, a Welsh missionary traveling in China at this time, remarked, "It was not safe to travel alone, for many of the starving had become cannibals." Richard noted that wolves and foxes grew fat on the hundreds of dead bodies that littered the roadsides. Eventually, some people ate sawdust, mud, and cakes made of ground stone particles. Most of these unfortunates died. As the disaster continued, some parents killed their own children to spare them a slow and painful death, then committed suicide. So many people died that officials buried the bodies in large communal pits, which became known as "ten-thousand-men holes."

Finally, in 1879 the rains returned to China. More than thirteen million people, over 10 percent of the country's population, had died of starvation, disease, and violence. In this way, nature provided a harsh, temporary solution to the country's problem of overpopulation.

Since the great Chinese famine, other societies have suffered from mass starvation brought on by the existence of too many people to feed. The latest incident began in the 1970s in the central African nations of Ethiopia, Chad, and Sudan. Famine is still widespread in sections of these desperately poor countries. Tens of thousands have died and millions continue to go hungry. In these societies, the lack of money and resources to properly feed, clothe, and house their inhabitants threatens to destroy the people and their environment.

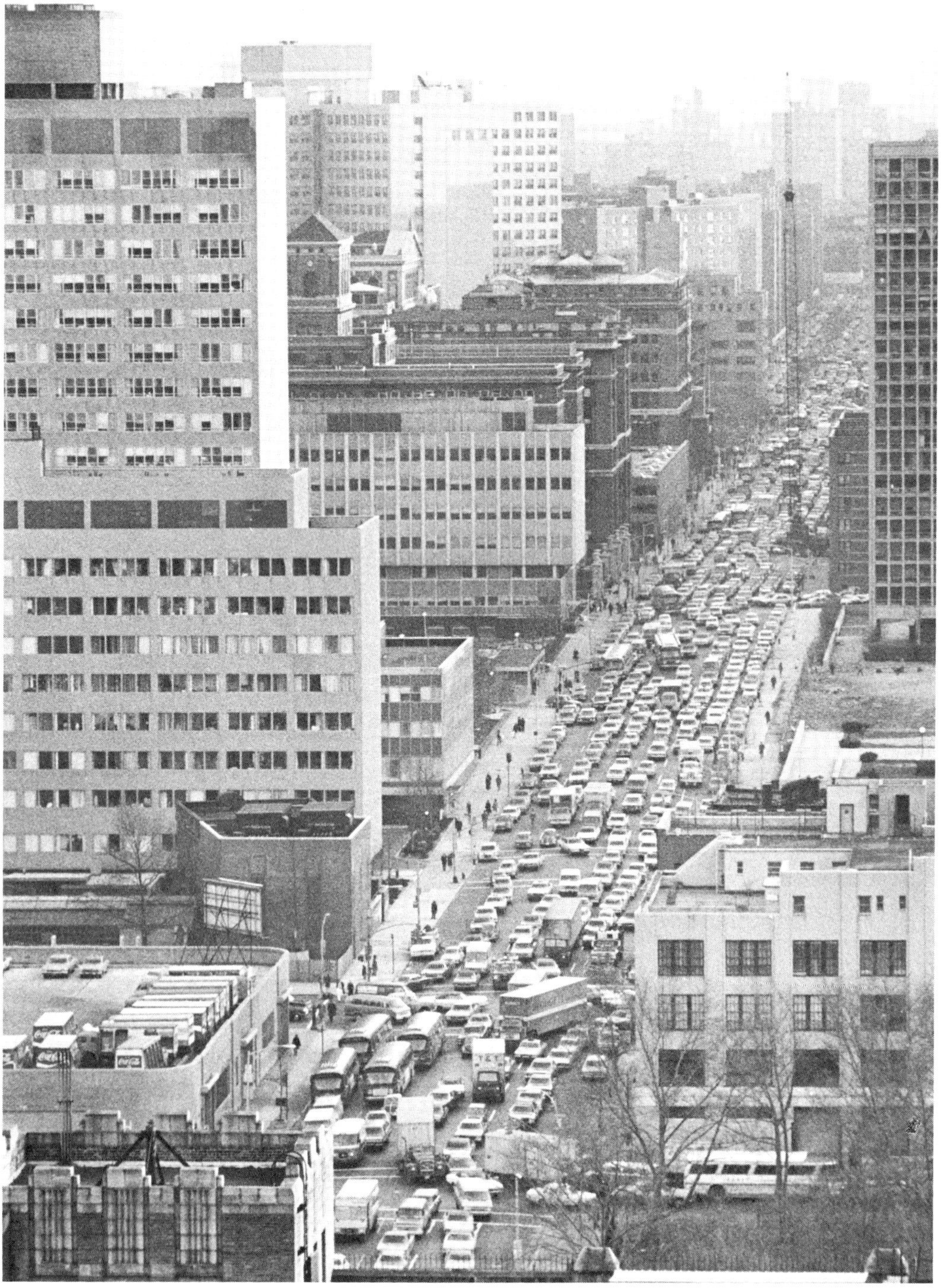

1
A Global Population Problem

THE WORLD'S HUMAN population has grown steadily over the centuries. In the year 1650, there were about 550 million people in the world, a little less than twice the present population of the United States. By 1990, the planet's population had risen to approximately 5.3 billion.

For most people, one billion is such a big number that it is difficult to imagine. Fortunately, the U.S. Population Reference Bureau in Washington, D.C., has suggested a way to help put huge population numbers in perspective. The bureau says to picture a large book with blank pages. Now imagine that each page is covered with tiny dots, each dot representing a single human being. There are 2,500 dots per square inch and 200,000 dots on an entire page.

Using this system, one page would just about hold the present population of the small city of Niagara Falls, New York. It would take a book 5,000 pages long to hold the dots for 1 billion people. To represent the 1990 world population of 5.3 billion, it would require a book 26,500 pages long,

(opposite page) A traffic jam in New York City. Most of the world's major cities face the problem of accommodating an ever-increasing population.

which would be a volume six feet thick.

The population of the planet is still rising. The jump from 550 million people in 1650 to 5.3 billion in 1990 represented an increase of nearly ten times in 340 years. At present, about 150 babies are born every minute. This means that the number of people added to the world's population each year is now about 90 million, more than all the people living in Mexico. And population experts, or demographers, expect the world's population to continue its dramatic rise well into the next century. According to the U.S. Bureau of the Census's *World Population Profile*, there will be about 8.7 billion people on earth by the year 2025 and more than 10 billion by 2040. That is enough people to populate fifty thousand cities the size of Niagara Falls.

Population growth and living standards

This rapid population growth has had and will continue to have important effects on the countries and peoples of the world. The most obvious effect of increased population is the increased demand for material goods and services. The more people there are in a country, the more food, housing, energy, and medical care that country needs in order to sustain its citizens.

At the moment, access to these goods and services is not a major problem in wealthy, industrialized countries such as the United States, Canada, and most European nations. These developed countries enjoy the use of many of the world's available resources and have high standards of living. Because of their wealth, developed countries can comfortably support relatively large populations. In 1990, about one billion people, or a bit less than one-fifth of the world's population, lived in developed countries.

By contrast, access to goods and services is

much more limited in poor, predominantly agricultural countries, like many in Latin America, central Africa, and Asia. These developing nations have little or no industry, few natural resources, and typically low living standards. In many developing countries, feeding and housing a growing population is a major problem. More than four billion people, over four-fifths of the world's population, lived in developing countries in 1990.

According to demographers, many of the developing nations suffer from overpopulation. A country, city, or other given area is overpopulated when there are not enough resources—such as food, housing, and energy—available to adequately support all the people who live in the area.

The problems of overpopulation

Many countries that are overpopulated are poor. They were poor before overpopulation and never had enough money and food for everyone. When their populations dramatically increase, their economies do not grow as fast and there is even

A fruit vendor in Senegal, Africa compared to a modern supermarket in a developed country (right). Most people in wealthy, industrialized countries enjoy an abundance of goods and services.

less to go around. The addition of more people simply makes these countries poorer. Hunger, low wages, a high rate of death for children, unsanitary living conditions, and disease plague these countries.

More than three-quarters of the world's people live in developing countries where the yearly income of an average family is two thousand dollars or less. This is the amount that a typical American two-car family spends each year on gasoline and oil changes. Yet even two thousand dollars a year would seem like a great deal of money to the world's poorest people. In 1990, the World Bank estimated that about one billion people lived in "absolute" poverty. This is defined as "being too poor to buy enough food to maintain health or

Starving children await food at a distribution center in Ethiopia. One out of every ten Ethiopian children dies, largely because of malnutrition.

perform a job." These absolute poor live in impoverished nations such as Ethiopia in north-central Africa and Bangladesh in southern Asia. For these people, "the march of human progress has become a retreat," according to the United Nations Children's Fund in 1989.

Developing countries like Ethiopia and Bangladesh have much higher rates of infant mortality, or child deaths, than developed countries like the United States, England, and the Soviet Union. In fact, one out of every ten children in Ethiopia dies by the age of six, mostly from hunger-related causes.

In poor, overpopulated countries, lack of food brings not only starvation but also diseases. In the first eighty years of the twentieth century, between twelve and fifteen million people died from such diseases. Aside from war, they were the world's leading cause of death. For instance, of the tens of thousands of people who perished when famine struck central Africa in the 1970s and 1980s, a high proportion died of tuberculosis and pneumonia. These diseases attacked mostly children and elderly people, who were already weak from malnutrition, or the lack of a proper diet.

A woman and schoolgirl get water from a community faucet in Tunisia, Africa.

Unsanitary living conditions

Other famine-related diseases are the result of unsanitary living conditions, which are common in poor, overpopulated areas. When there is not enough clean water to support a population, for example, many people resort to drinking contaminated water. This was the cause of cholera outbreaks that killed thousands of people in several Indian cities in the 1960s and 1970s. Similarly, in areas where population is high and food scarce, desperate people often eat food that is moldy or has been contaminated with bacteria.

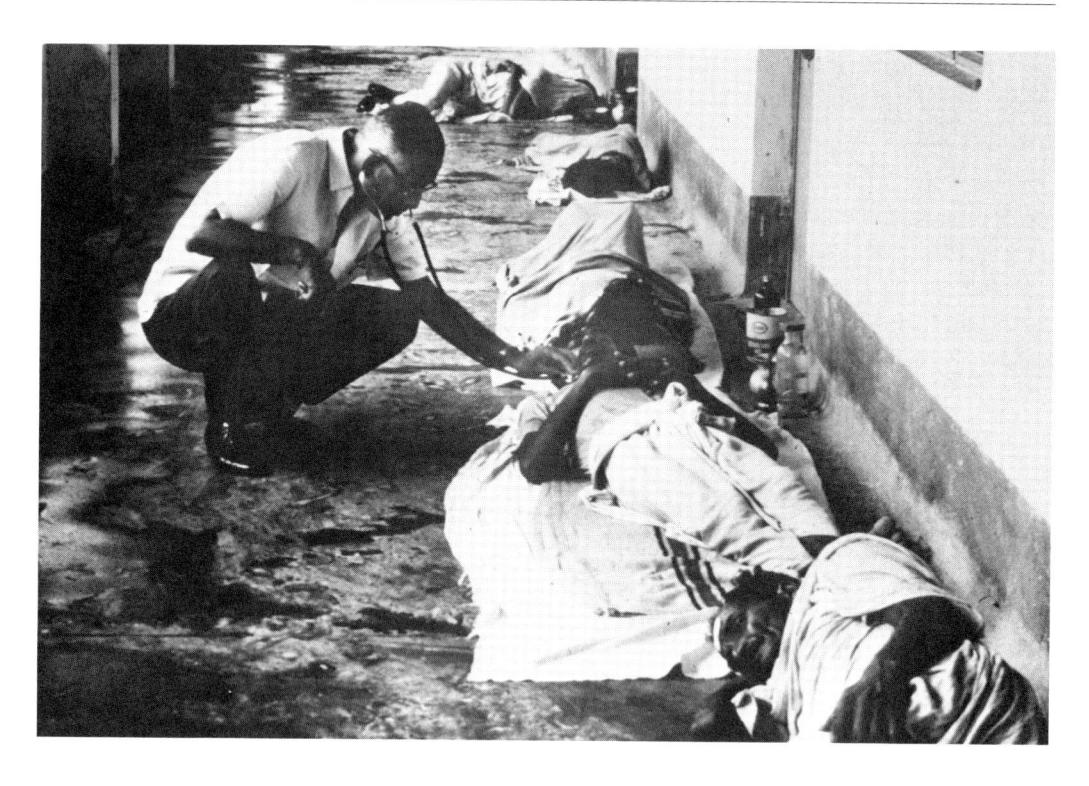

A doctor examines cholera victims in a hospital compound in Calcutta, India. Cholera broke out in the 1960s and 1970s when people drank contaminated water.

Two of the leading causes of death in the African famine of the 1970s were enteritis and diarrhea, infections caused by eating contaminated food.

When there are too many mouths to feed

What is it like to live in a country that is too poor to support the majority of its people? Population researcher Dom Moraes visited Colombia, a developing country in the northern section of South America. He spent some time in Vista Hermosa, a suburb of the city of Bogota. Like more than 80 percent of Colombian towns, Vista Hermosa is a slum, composed almost entirely of poorly constructed wooden shacks. Some of the shacks have electricity and running water, but most do not. Broken windows and rotten roofing planks are a common sight. All the roads leading to and inside the town are unpaved. As he entered the decaying, poverty-stricken town, Moraes sadly observed that Vista Hermosa did not live up to its name, which means "beautiful view."

One of the first things Moraes noticed was how filthy the town appeared. Empty food cans littered many roadsides, and burro droppings cluttered the grassy areas. "We saw children drawing water from the well that served the village," said Moraes. "It was the color of excrement [human waste], its surface . . . afloat with insects and tiny brown crumbs of decay."

Too many people, too few jobs

Moraes learned that most of the residents who had jobs worked as construction workers in nearby Bogota, earning an average of twenty dollars a month. Nearly one-third of the inhabitants of the town were unemployed. "There are too many people and too few jobs," a local official told Moraes. "No one believes there will be many more jobs next year or the year after that," he added. "But the people continue to have huge families . . . eight, ten, twelve children or more. Is it a wonder that we have so much filth and poverty?"

To prove his point, the official led Moraes to the one-room shack of a woman named Georgina de Torres, whose life of poverty had obviously taken its toll. "I took her to be about fifty," said Moraes. "She turned out to be thirty-five, and she had had sixteen children, nine of whom had died." The official explained that diarrhea, vomiting, and pneumonia had killed the children. The surviving children "were sprawled out on mattresses, and one of them, who was two years old, had tiny, deformed legs . . . and, his mother told me, couldn't walk," Moraes recalled.

Mrs. Torres explained that her husband is a construction worker who drinks heavily and never talks to her. The official added that "when he is

In Hong Kong, a young boy eats lunch on the doorstep of his home, beside an open sewer that drains raw sewage into a nearby harbor.

In Cairo, Egypt, two children play in front of the deteriorating apartment building where they live. Many poor countries lack the money and resources to adequately house their citizens.

drunk, he beats her, and he beats the children, even the babies." The woman sadly told Moraes that she wanted to leave her husband, buy decent clothes and food for the children, and even send some of them to school. But that would take money, and there was no way she would ever have any. "I only went to school for three months," she said. "But even I know that people should live better. How can you live better than animals if you do not even know that you are able to be people?"

The ability to sustain life

Georgina de Torres, her children, and her neighbors are only a few of the hundreds of millions of people living in squalor in developing countries around the world. While these people suffer from hunger, disease, and other problems of overcrowding, most of the citizens of developed countries, which often have far larger populations, lead relatively prosperous lives. Rapid increases in population do not automatically lead to poverty and misery. Examining a poor country and a wealthy one side by side illustrates that there are two ways population growth can affect a country.

For example, compare two small countries with large populations—Ethiopia and Japan. Ethiopia, with a population of about fifty million people, is an extremely poor, agriculturally based country. Ethiopians still use the same primitive methods of farming that their ancestors used. The country has no industry and no money to purchase more advanced farming technology. Therefore, Ethiopians are unable to increase the amount of food they grow, while their population continues to expand. The average Ethiopian makes the equivalent of about $110 per year and is barely able to find the food needed to sustain life.

Japan, on the other hand, is a developed, highly industrialized country with a population of nearly

FOOD FOR THOUGHT

A farmer plows his field in Ethiopia. Although the economy of the country is based on agriculture, lack of money and technology forces the Ethiopians to use primitive farming methods.

125 million people. The nation has a very high population density, which means that a large number of people live in a relatively small area. Judged solely by the number and density of its inhabitants, Japan should be even poorer than Ethiopia. Yet this is not the case. Japan boasts a strong, healthy economy. It produces and exports a wide variety of consumer goods such as cars, audio equipment, and high technology that many other industrialized nations want. Japan's success in the world trade market allows the vast majority of Japanese to enjoy comfortable living standards. The average Japanese person earns about twenty-two thousand dollars a year. Because of its relatively high income, Japan, unlike Ethiopia, can afford to import the food and material goods it lacks.

Having a future to look forward to

The difference in the economies of developed and developing countries is also clearly illustrated by comparing New Zealand, an island country in the Pacific Ocean, and Nicaragua, a small nation in Central America. Both of these countries had populations of about 3.5 million people in 1990. Both economies were agriculturally based. But the ability of these countries to sustain these populations was very different. Because New Zealand, like Japan, possesses industry and advanced technology, it earns a great deal of money through trade with other nations. This wealth, combined with the country's native resources, such as reserves of precious metals, allows it to feed and clothe the majority of its people.

By contrast, Nicaragua lacks industry, technology, and natural resources. It earns far less money through trade than New Zealand. In addition, Nicaragua has suffered from repressive governments and disruptive civil war. The swiftly rising population of Nicaragua is already beginning to suffer from the effects of overpopulation. Many people in Nicaragua are not able to earn enough

In Mexico City, families hang out their wash in a decaying alley.

money for food and shelter. New Zealand on the other hand, could possibly support a much larger population than it currently does. Its economy continues to expand. There are more jobs, more housing, and more food available each year than the present population uses.

More opportunities

Affluent, or wealthy, countries offer their citizens many more opportunities than do poorer, overpopulated nations. While nearly half the people in Nicaragua face a future as hopeless as that of Colombia's Georgina de Torres, the vast majority of New Zealand's citizens can look forward to lives of relative comfort and productivity.

New Zealand's economy and government resemble those of the United States. Other successful countries that resemble the United States are Canada, Australia, and some European nations. Since these nations manage their economies well, most of their people have high standards of living. Researcher Shirley Hartley explains, "These are the most enviable regions of the world: they have large territories well supplied with known resources; populations of small or moderate size; an advanced, rapidly expanding technology; skilled personnel . . . they have the trading or purchasing power to augment [increase] their desired standards of living."

With strong economies, advanced technology, and plenty of natural resources, these developed countries do not have as much of a problem supporting their growing populations.

In this way, the peoples of the world are divided between the rich and the poor, the well-fed and the undernourished. Some people have the chance, through hard work, to create happy, meaningful lives. Many others in the developing countries around the world work hard merely to survive.

A couple relaxes by the whirlpool at their luxury condominium in Miami, Florida. The United States and other countries with vast industry and technology offer their citizens many comforts and conveniences.

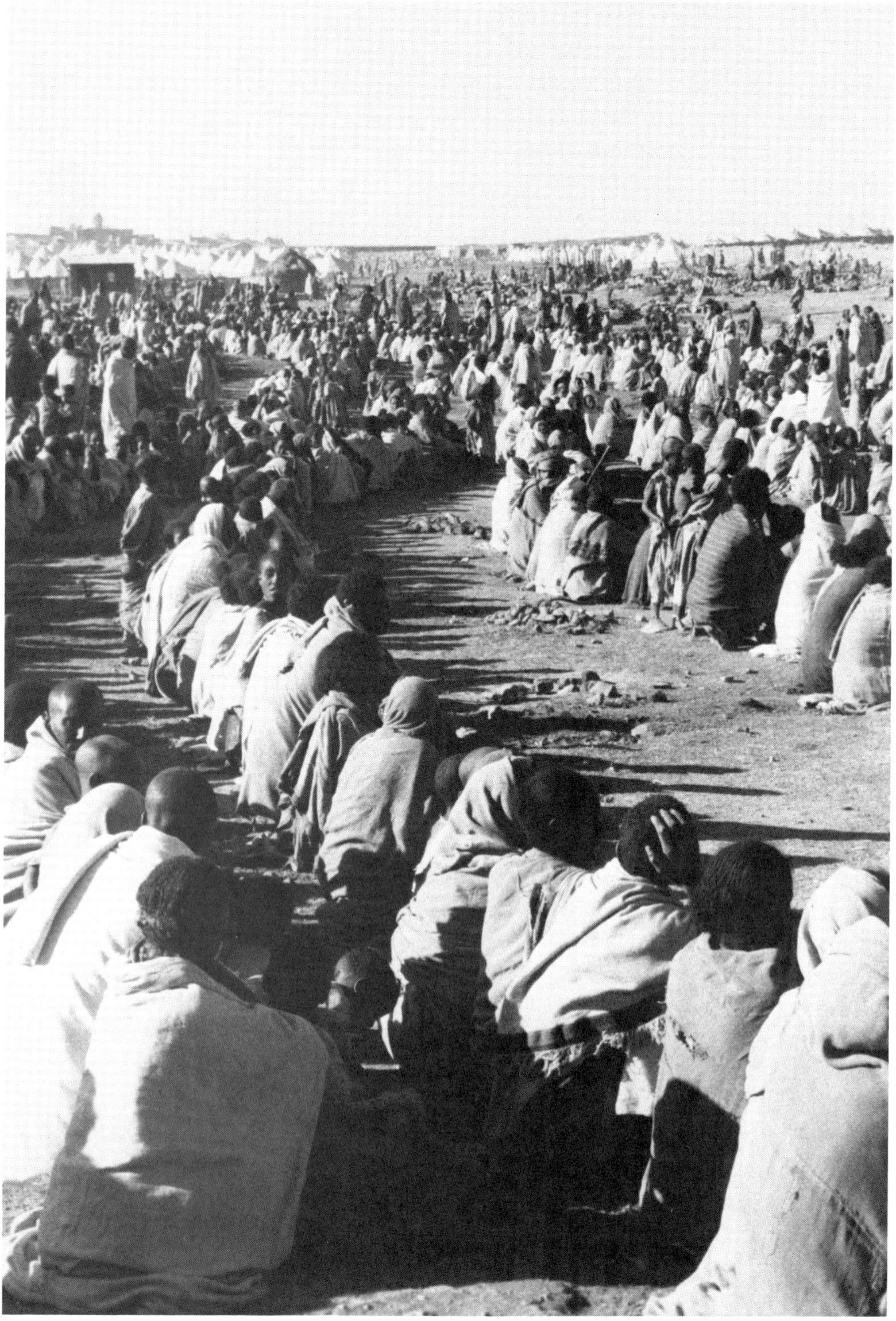

2
The Developing Countries

THE WORLD'S DEVELOPING countries are often referred to as the Third World. Because these nations usually cannot adequately support their populations, the people in them often suffer from the overpopulation problems of poverty, hunger, and disease. In addition, these countries have little advanced technology and few natural resources, so they must import many essential products and raw materials from more prosperous countries. These items include basic resources such as oil, chemicals, metals, and many foods. Developing countries usually have weak economies and little money and they cannot afford to import enough of these goods and materials to maintain a decent standard of living for all their citizens. Many of the goods they do import have to be bought on credit. As a result, most developing countries owe large debts to wealthier nations.

A majority of the people in developing nations fall into two general groups. They are either poor farmers living in backward villages in the countryside or impoverished workers dwelling in the slums of large, overcrowded cities. Most people are poorly educated and do not have access to basic medical care. There are, however, some people

(opposite page) At a relief shelter in Ethiopia, thousands of famine victims wait for the distribution of blankets.

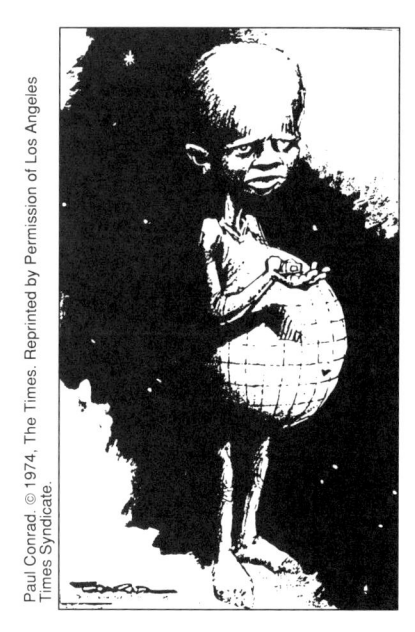

in Third World countries who are well-off or even wealthy. These individuals represent an extreme minority in these nations. In fact, the wealth of many Third World nations is concentrated among these elite few, while the majority of the population is desperately poor.

Locating developing nations

Developing countries are found in many areas of the world. Located in southern Asia, India, Pakistan, and Bangladesh are the most populous Third World nations. In 1990, more than one-fifth of the world's people lived in these three countries. Farther to the east are other developing Asian countries like Vietnam, Cambodia, and the island nation of Indonesia. Most African countries are classified as part of the Third World; the poorest ones are Ethiopia, Uganda, Chad, and Sudan, all in the central area of the continent. In South and Central America, Colombia, Peru, Nicaragua, El Salvador, and the island country of Haiti are among the poorer developing nations.

A few members of the Third World have developed some industry and technical capabilities. For this reason, they are sometimes referred

Exhausted after walking for days to reach a relief shelter, an elderly Ethiopian rests his head. Ethiopia is an example of a country that lacks the necessary technology and resources to sustain its population.

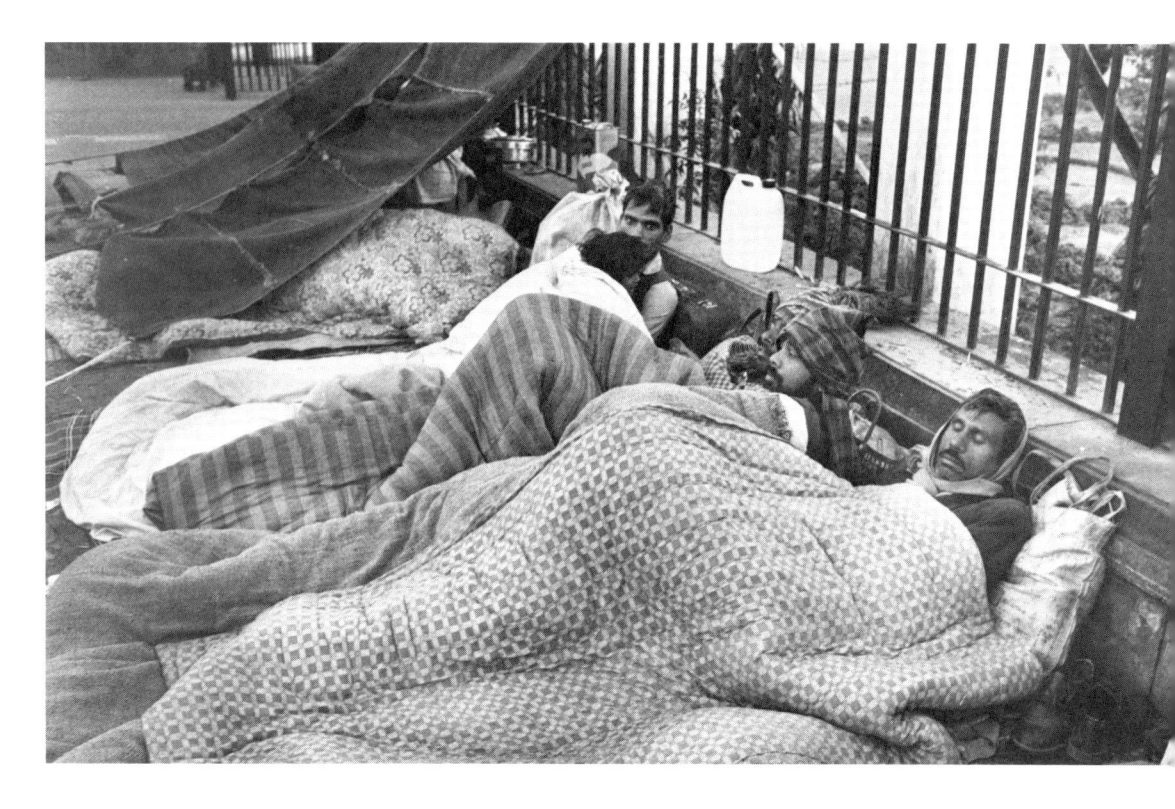

In India, homeless men prepare for another cold night on a New Delhi street.

to as semideveloped countries. But because their populations are large and their economies weak, a majority of their citizens still live in conditions of severe poverty. So many population experts continue to categorize these nations as developing. Mexico and Brazil are the most notable examples.

Substandard living conditions

Because the economies and resources of most developing nations cannot keep pace with their rapidly growing populations, average living conditions in these countries are often miserable. For instance, in the Indian cities of Calcutta, Bombay, and Delhi, huge numbers of people literally have no roof over their heads. In 1989, the Indian government released a report estimating that 2.5 million Indians now live out their entire lives in the streets.

Population researcher Pranay Gupte studied the

effects of overpopulation in India during the 1970s and 1980s. He observed that basic facilities that are taken for granted in places like the United States are defective or even nonexistent in most parts of India. According to Gupte, 65 percent of the people in India have no tap water and must use nearby rivers for drinking, bathing, and washing clothes. At least 37 percent of the people have no electricity. Gupte was especially shocked that up to half of the people have no toilet facilities. These unfortunate individuals, he said, must defecate in alleys and vacant lots or into pots that are then emptied into the streets.

Gupte pointed out that the construction of new water, electrical, and sanitary facilities does not happen fast enough to meet the needs of India's rapidly expanding population. So more and more people must share existing facilities. This problem is most obvious in India's cities, "which are already horrendously overcrowded," Gupte observed.

Indian women bathe and wash clothes in a river near their homes. Population researcher Pranay Gupte estimates that 65 percent of the people in India have no tap water.

Bombay

As an example, Gupte cited Bombay, the country's second-largest city. In 1990, Bombay had a population of nearly 12 million. The city's population density was 120,300 people per square mile. Eliminating the space taken up by streets, stores, and public buildings, that amounts to a total living space of roughly eight square feet for each person. With people crowded so closely together, it is difficult to imagine how the population of the city could continue to grow. Yet it does. Presently, Bombay's population is increasing by several thousand people a week. The situation is similar in other poor developing nations. Gupte called this situation "alarming," saying: "I don't know where all these people are going to live. In the developing countries themselves, the large cities are already bursting at the seams. Anyone who's been to Lagos [in Nigeria, Africa] or Mexico City or Shanghai or Bombay or Jakarta [in Indonesia] or Cairo [in Egypt] will know what overcrowded cities are all about: filth, and crime and chaos and decay and disorder."

To determine where all these people will live, Gupte and other researchers studied the housing situation in India. They found that in the near future, most of the new members of Indian society will end up living in the same places where their parents do now. This is because the government builds very little housing for low- or no-income families. For example, according to the Indian publication *Business World*, most of the residential buildings constructed in the 1980s or now being built in Bombay are luxury skyscrapers. These cater to India's tiny but powerful wealthy class

Shantytowns, like this one in New Delhi, India, house thousands of people who would otherwise live on the streets.

and to foreign businesspeople. One-bedroom apartments in these buildings sell for $100,000 or more. Obviously, the poor cannot afford these accommodations.

Instead, many of the poorest families end up in *chawls*, filthy, densely inhabited tenement buildings. In a typical *chawl*, as many as one dozen people live in each room, and often, one hundred people or more share a common latrine, a toilet without plumbing. Many others, finding the *chawls* full, resort to living in shantytowns, which are clusters of wooden shacks, or even in sewer pipes.

When interviewed by a population researcher and a social worker in 1984, Shaila Pyarelal and her eight children had been living in a Bombay drainage pipe for four years. Before that, they had lived in a *chawl* with Shaila's husband, a janitor in downtown Bombay. When he fell from an overcrowded commuter train and died, Shaila could no longer afford to stay in the *chawl* and set up resi-

Children play in a stagnant, littered pool in a Mexican slum, exposing themselves to diseases such as typhoid and dysentery.

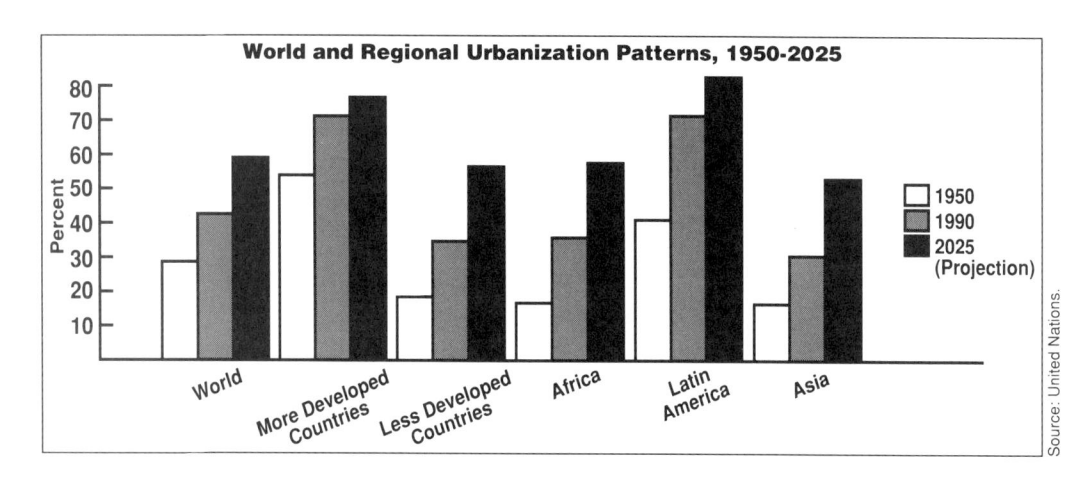

World and Regional Urbanization Patterns, 1950-2025

Source: United Nations.

dence in the abandoned pipe. She managed to buy food with money she earned working as a maid for middle-class families in a more affluent part of the city. She also begged for money from passersby. Each day, people from other parts of the city or from the countryside arrived and tried to crowd into the shacks and sewer pipes surrounding Shaila's own makeshift home. But residents of the area formed patrols to force the newcomers away.

Shaila blamed her situation on her own ignorance. She said that she and her husband moved to Bombay from a poor rural town because they heard things were much better in the city. "Had we known things were so bad here," she commented, "we wouldn't have come at all."

Cinturon de Miseria

Shaila's predicament is not an uncommon one in Third World countries. On the outskirts of Mexico City, Hilda Vasquez and her four children live in a run-down shack in an area known as *Cinturon de Miseria* (the Belt of Misery). These overcrowded, disease-ridden neighborhoods are the fastest growing parts of Mexico City. Originally, Hilda and her husband lived on a farm in the countryside. They could barely make a living, and like the Pyarelals in India, they moved to the city in search of jobs. Unfortunately, Hilda's husband abandoned her and the children only a few days after they settled in Mexico City.

Hilda works in a tortilla factory and earns about four dollars a day. This is even less than she and her husband made on the farm, and she complains that she can never make ends meet. Sometimes, her oldest children earn extra money for the family by polishing shoes in city alleyways.

Hilda finds living conditions in the *Cinturon de Miseria* horrendous. Electricity and running water are available only occasionally, and homes in the area are constantly broken into by thieves and vandals. There is no heat during the winter. There are so many people without proper toilet facilities in the district that human waste piles up in alleys and vacant lots. When the wastes dry out, the wind carries them in the form of a "fecal snow" that falls over Hilda's neighborhood. Hepatitis, a disease that can be contracted by contact with fecal material, is common in the district.

The city versus the countryside

Hilda, like Shaila, learned too late that moving to the city was a mistake. "I wish I could tell all those people who keep flocking to Mexico City not to come, that there aren't any jobs here, that the magic of the city is an illusion, but these people keep coming. The city keeps growing. What will happen to us?" Hilda asked.

Hilda's and Shaila's stories illustrate that, in the world's poorest nations, it matters little whether one lives in a city or in the countryside. Poverty and the effects of overpopulation are everywhere. The rural areas strain to supply enough food and resources for the growing population. The desperate rural poor flee to the cities, believing the rumors that there are plenty of jobs available. The

Ethiopian farmers plow the land the old-fashioned way.

In Ethiopia, would-be passengers clamor for bus tickets. Because of an inadequate transportation system, the bus conductor is able to sell tickets to only a fraction of the people.

rumors turn out to be false.

As the cities draw increasing numbers of people from the countryside, the already overcrowded conditions get worse. Housing, transportation, water, and electricity become more and more scarce. Most population experts see no end in sight to these problems. They say that by the year 2000 there will be sixty-five cities in the world with populations of five million or more. Mexico City, already the most populous city on earth, will have twenty-six million inhabitants, and India's nine largest cities will have a combined total of seventy-nine million people.

The growing hunger problem

Overcrowding, unsanitary conditions, homelessness, and the flight of rural poor into the cities are all serious problems associated with overpopulation in developing countries. But probably the most devastating population-related problem is hunger.

Children in a squatters' camp near Cape Town in South Africa pose for the camera. Squatters—people who illegally occupy land because they have no home—live under the constant threat of forced removal.

Malnutrition and starvation affect vast numbers of people around the world. According to studies made by the United Nations and the World Bank, nearly one billion people in 1990 were too poor to grow or buy the food they needed. That is about one out of every five of the earth's inhabitants. These people, most of whom lived in poor developing nations, did not eat enough protein or vitamins and minerals essential to good health.

Of these absolute poor, two-fifths, or about 400 million people, were so hungry that their health was severely threatened or their growth stunted. Most of these were children. Experts estimate that two out of every ten children in developing countries stay hungry for most of their lives. Sally Struthers, chairperson of the Christian Children's Fund says, "Unfortunately, I've seen what malnutrition does to the children of the Third World. In Guatemala [in Central America], Thailand [in southeast Asia], Kenya [in Africa] and Uganda

World Population Growth 1750-2100

Total world population

Developing regions

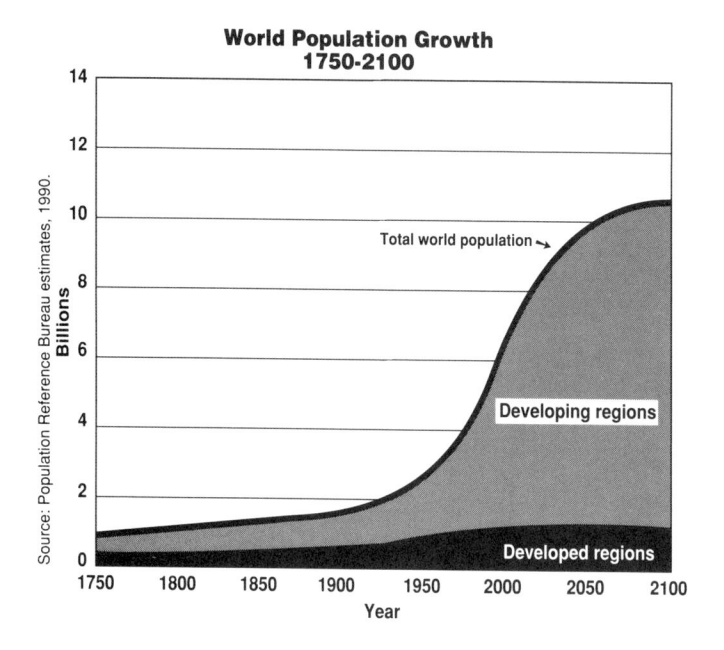

Developed regions

Source: Population Reference Bureau estimates, 1990.

I've looked into the tired eyes of malnourished youngsters who have forever lost the chance to grow straight and strong."

Starvation contributes heavily to infant mortality in these nations. "More than fourteen million Third World children under the age of five ... die each year because they are too poor to be healthy," comments Struthers. This high rate of child death, in turn, often affects family size. Parents expect that some of their children will die of hunger or starvation-related diseases, so they try to compensate by having large families. This practice further expands the population, creating even more poverty.

For example, in the small country of Gabon, on the west coast of Africa, malnutrition is common and infant mortality high. F. Nguema Ndong, the former minister of social affairs, complains that the population of his country is rising too rapidly. There is more and more malnutrition, he says, and too many children dying from it. As many as ten out of every one hundred children die before their second birthday, so couples keep having huge families. "My eldest brother," says Ndong, "has . . . seventeen children. But my second brother has . . . twenty children." Ndong realizes that this only creates more mouths to feed. But many of his people are uneducated and resist new ideas that go against traditional views about having children.

The increasing malnutrition in Gabon and other Third World countries is directly related to rapid population growth. The problem of too many people and too little food makes it difficult for these nations to improve their living conditions.

Overpopulation and the food supply

Population scientists usually measure a society's ability to support its population adequately by the success of its efforts to feed its people. Tragically, in the world's poorest countries, the more populations expand, the less successful such efforts become.

This connection between population growth and the food supply was first recognized and described by the British economist Thomas Robert Malthus (1766-1834). In his 1798 book, *An Essay on the Principle of Population*, Malthus argued that human population always grows faster than the food supply. According to this view, increases in food production cannot keep pace with increases in population. Eventually, there is not enough food to go around and people begin to starve. Famine is one of the ways that nature keeps human populations from getting too large, according to Malthus. Disease and war also work to reduce the excess population. He called these factors natural checks against population growth.

Modern researchers believe that Malthus described only part of the problem of hunger in human society. In addition to lack of food, they say,

In the eighteenth century, British economist Thomas Robert Malthus argued that human population will always grow faster than food supply.

A relief worker helps an Ethiopian refugee weigh her child. If the child's weight is below a critical level, he will be put on an emergency feeding program.

there is another problem often associated with poor, overpopulated countries—inefficient food distribution. Developing countries often suffer from small and ineffective transportation networks and poor management of existing food supplies.

A classic example of this problem occurred in the great Chinese famine in the late 1870s. During the crisis, many other countries donated food to the starving Chinese. But getting that food from the port cities to hungry farm families proved difficult. China's poverty-stricken masses were spread out over the vast rural countryside. Most of these areas were far from the ports, and the few existing roads into the interior of the country were badly in need of repair. There were not enough horses and wagons to carry the food. And gangs of thieves stole much of what the government managed to transport.

To make matters worse, there were so many hungry people that the government could not keep track of their numbers and whereabouts. So no one was sure how much food to ship and where to ship it. As a result, the government found it nearly impossible to get food and other relief supplies to those who needed them.

As in China, many of the recent efforts to relieve the hunger in Ethiopia have been hampered by mismanagement, poor transportation networks, and violence. Roads and railroad lines in the region are poorly maintained or even nonexistent. And often, there are not enough trucks to carry food from one area to another. In addition, there

African relief workers separate bags of grain that will be distributed to the hungry.

was a bloody civil war in Ethiopia in the 1980s. Armies on both sides used existing food supplies as a weapon, keeping the food from reaching the poorest people who needed it most. Violence also erupted in the neighboring country of Sudan in 1988. There, despite an all-out farming effort, as well as tons of food donations from foreign countries, 100,000 people died from famine-related causes.

Each day thousands of children are born into societies that lack the means to support them. Each week more and more Shaila Pyarelals seek shelter in rotting shacks and drainage pipes. Their children appear doomed to live a life of poverty and hunger as the populations of the world's developing countries relentlessly expand. Yet, even as these tragedies unfold, people in other societies enjoy lives of comfort and plenty. They grow up taking for granted things like adequate food and housing, hot and cold running water, and abundant electricity and other forms of energy. The world they know is very different from the one inhabited by the children of Ethiopia or the slum dwellers of Bombay. How can this be? How can some nations, with populations equal to or even larger than those of developing countries, escape the ravages of hunger, disease, and high infant mortality?

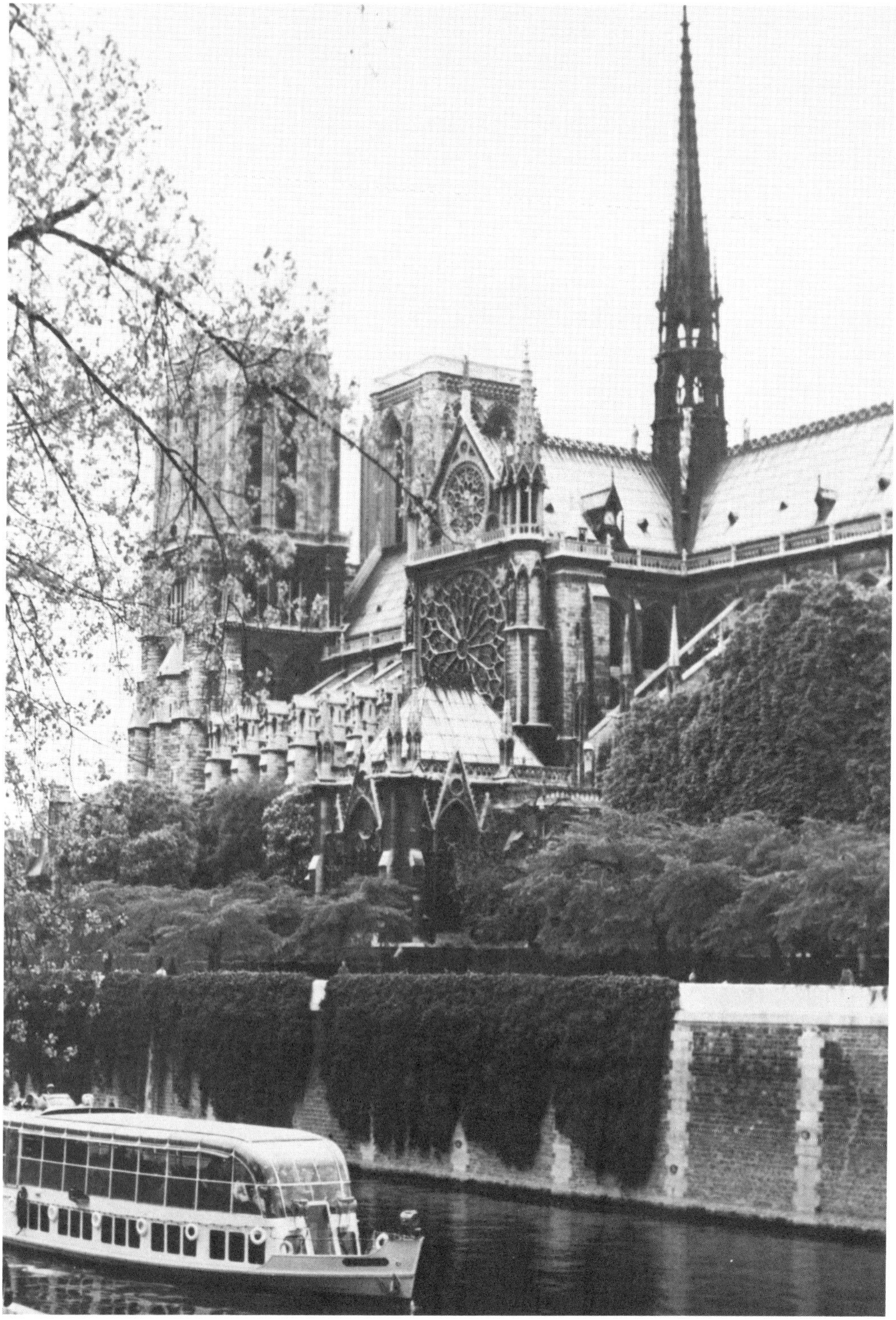

3

The Developed Countries

THE DEVELOPED COUNTRIES of the world are able to adequately support the majority of their citizens. These nations include the United States, Canada, Britain, Australia, and New Zealand. France, Germany, the Netherlands, and most of the other Western European nations are developed, as are the Scandinavian countries, the Soviet Union, and Japan. Poverty, hunger, and homelessness occur in these countries, but those that suffer from these conditions represent a tiny minority of the population. For the most part, people in the developed countries are not affected by starvation, disease, and other common problems associated with overpopulation.

A wealth of goods and resources

The developing countries are highly industrialized, with many factories, power plants, and mechanized forms of transportation. They have advanced technologies and machines and a large force of trained technicians to operate them. The developed countries have access to or can purchase vast amounts of natural resources such as oil, coal, and natural gas for energy production. They also have or can afford to buy large deposits

(opposite page) Developed countries are able to support the majority of their citizens through industry, technology, and access to natural resources. France, pictured here, is just one example.

of iron, aluminum, diamonds, uranium, and other important raw materials.

With an abundance of basic resources and the industrial capacity to use them, the wealthy countries produce tremendous amounts of manufactured goods. These include advanced farming devices such as tractors, harvesters, and milking machines. These countries also produce time- and work-saving devices for the home, including washing machines and driers, vacuum cleaners, and food processors. In addition, most homes in developed countries are equipped with entertainment devices such as televisions, stereo systems, video recorders, and home computers. Almost all of these items, which are considered luxuries in Third World countries, are taken for granted in developed nations.

Developed countries produce these and thous-

With advanced farming equipment, farmers in developed countries can harvest an abundance of food.

A mother feeds her seven children with food purchased with food stamps. The U.S. food stamp program provides disadvantaged households with stamps or coupons that can be used to buy food.

ands of other goods and services because of great popular demand. People demand the products because they can afford them. The economies of these nations are strong, so most people are employed and wages are generally high. For instance, in 1990, the yearly per capita income—the amount of money made by an average person in one year—in the United States was about seventeen thousand dollars. In comparison, Nicaragua's per capita income was about seven hundred dollars, and India's was three hundred dollars.

Because they have more money, the residents of developed countries have immensely better living standards than most people in developing nations. Average living conditions in the United States, France, Japan, and other affluent countries meet certain minimum standards. For instance, supplies of water are treated to remove impurities, and sanitation systems treat and remove wastes to maintain a reasonable state of health for nearly all citizens. Education is usually well-organized, as are various welfare programs that reach out to most of the disadvantaged. Even the poorest people in developed countries usually enjoy the regular use of electricity, flush toilets, refrigerators,

A stream of cars pours across the Golden Gate Bridge in San Francisco, California. The number of automobiles on American roads continues to increase.

and televisions. The developed countries adequately support relatively large numbers of people and generally avoid the destructive effects of overpopulation.

Unequal shares of the resource pie

The way people in wealthy countries live has an indirect effect on how people in poorer countries live. This is because the developed countries play an important part in shaping the world economy, which in turn affects poor, overpopulated countries. Usually, the developed countries are able to compete more successfully than the developing countries for needed resources.

Maintaining high standards of living in developing nations is expensive, not only in terms of money but also in terms of energy and resources. In order to keep these standards high for their constantly growing populations, the developed countries must find, extract, and use huge amounts of natural resources. For instance, countries like the United States, Germany, and the Soviet Union depend heavily on fossil fuels like oil, natural gas, and coal for their massive yearly energy needs.

Since they can afford to mine or import such resources in abundance, developed nations end up using a much larger share of the world's supply of these commodities than developing nations do. In fact, the wealthiest countries, with a small percentage of the world's population, use nearly all of the resources developed in the world each year.

For example, according to studies made by the World Bank and other organizations, the United States has less than 5 percent of the world's population yet uses more than 30 percent of the world's energy-producing fuels. The average American uses seven times as much energy as the average non-American. The number of cars and trucks on American roads increases by more than four million per year, and more than one million new homes are built each year in the United States. Since all of these vehicles and houses "consume" energy-producing fuels like oil and gas, experts expect U.S. demand for these fuels to continue to increase.

This does not mean that the United States and other wealthy countries purposely keep poorer countries from getting and using vital resources. Poor nations simply cannot afford to compete successfully for resources on the world market. Usually, even if these countries have natural resources, they are too poor to buy and operate the machinery needed to extract them. In comparison to developed nations, these struggling, impoverished countries are also energy-poor. For example, in 1986, an average resident of Sudan used only 1/40 the amount of energy used by an average Japanese and only 1/100 the amount used by an average American.

By calculating and studying statistics like these, population researchers can learn about the relationship between resource consumption and overpopulation. One conclusion is that the countries with a wide variety of resources at their disposal are able to adequately support large numbers of people without becoming overpopulated.

Tens of thousands of Japanese do their holiday shopping in Tokyo's downtown Ginza. Japan is another example of a developed country that can support most of its citizens.

Prosperity with few resources?

But this relationship is not always so straightforward. For example, some countries lack nearly all essential resources but still manage to maintain good living standards. Often, this is possible when a country has large supplies of one particular valuable resource that can be traded to other nations.

Consider the case of Saudi Arabia. The country is composed mainly of vast stretches of desert with very little fertile soil and fresh water. So the Saudis cannot grow all the food they need to sus-

Workers maintain an oil rig in Saudi Arabia. The sale of natural resources such as oil to the industrial world is the lifeline of many countries.

tain their present population. The country has small deposits of iron ore and copper but not nearly enough to maintain a robust economy. The Saudis also lack supplies of most other important resources.

Luckily for the Saudis, they have huge reserves of oil, far more oil than they need for their own use. In 1980, Saudi Arabia produced nearly 500 million tons of oil, about twenty times more than the United States, also a major oil producer. And in 1990, the Saudis discovered a vast new oil deposit that promises to expand their production by as much as 20 percent for five years or more.

The Saudis earn large sums of money by exporting their excess oil to other nations. With this money, they then pay to import all the necessary food and other resources they lack. Because they are fortunate enough to live above large deposits of oil, the Saudis can support a population well beyond what they could otherwise. In fact, they can presently afford to increase their population significantly and still maintain very high living standards.

How the Dutch import prosperity

Another example of a country with a large population but few native resources is that of the Netherlands. This tiny Western European country is only half the size of the state of New Jersey. Yet in 1990, the Netherlands had a population of about fifteen million people, more than twice as many people as New Jersey. And the Netherlands had an average population density of nearly eleven hundred people per square mile. So there are a great many Dutch living in a very small area.

The Netherlands has very little fertile land and few native minerals. And there is no oil, coal, or uranium for energy production. The Dutch did discover and develop a large field of natural gas in the northern section of their country in the 1970s, but that supply is expected to run out within fifteen to twenty years. For the most part, the Netherlands is a resource-poor nation with a natural carrying capacity of no more than one or two million people. Carrying capacity is the population that an area can support without experiencing any of the physical damage to the environment or other problems that come with overpopulation. Despite this handicap, the Netherlands manages to support its fifteen million people with a standard of living equal to most of the world's richest nations.

Like Saudi Arabia, the Netherlands is able to exceed its natural carrying capacity by importing essential materials. For instance, according to the World Resource Institute, between 1984 and 1986 the Netherlands imported nearly four million tons of cereals, 130,000 tons of plant oils, and 480,000 tons of peas and beans. The Dutch use a large percentage of these and other products to feed their cattle. Much of the milk and meat produced—330,000 tons of milk and 1.2 million tons of meat—was then exported. Because the prices charged for the exports were much higher than the prices paid for the original imports, the Dutch made a handsome profit. This money helps keep their standard of living high.

The Dutch also import all of their fuel oil and nearly all of their iron, copper, tin, and other minerals. In addition, because there are few forests in the country, they import almost all their wood and paper products. In a sense, the Dutch import their fresh water, too. They get nearly all of it from the Rhine River, which flows into the Netherlands from the mountains of Switzerland and Germany. To get the resources to keep their population living prosperously, the Dutch are almost totally dependent on other nations.

While it may seem that the Dutch lead a precarious existence by being so dependent, they really do not. The Dutch have a strong, stable democratic government that controls the flow of imports and exports in a highly efficient manner.

This stability helps the Dutch to maintain their present prosperity.

An abundance of food

One of the most dramatic differences between developed and undeveloped nations is the ability to feed large numbers of people. For the most part, hunger is not a major problem in developed countries. According to studies made by the United Nations and the World Bank, in 1990, about 1 billion of the world's 5.3 billion people were "very well fed." Almost all of them lived in large, affluent countries like the United States, Canada, Australia, and France. These nations are rich in fertile soil and fresh water, the components necessary for growing large amounts of crops and raising livestock. They also possess the money and technology necessary for developing advanced machinery and the fertilizers needed to generate plentiful harvests.

The very well-fed also live in tiny affluent countries such as Luxembourg, located between Germany and France; Bahrain, in the Middle East; and Monaco on the south coast of Europe. Like Saudi Arabia and the Netherlands, these lands have little fertile land and water for irrigation and are barely able to grow enough food to adequately support their populations. Judged solely by these criteria, they should be poverty-stricken and overpopulated. Yet they are not. This is because they have earned a great deal of money from international banking and other business ventures. They can afford to buy all the food they need from other nations.

When a country has an abundance of food, it is a

'We can't seem to keep our heads above water'...

sure indication that the nation can support a large population with high living standards. Population scientists use food to measure the success of a society in a number of ways. One way is to observe how much its citizens spend on food. In general, the countries in which people spend the smallest proportion of their income on food are the countries with the highest living standards. Obviously, the less a person is forced to spend for food, the more he or she can spend on other things. This is why people in the developed countries can afford to own so many material goods. For example, in the United States, the average family spends about 17 to 18 percent of its yearly income on food. That leaves 82 to 83 percent of the family's money that can be spent on clothes, housing, and luxuries. By contrast, an average Indian family spends 67 percent of its income on food.

Food variety is another measure of a country's success. People in wealthy countries like the United States and Great Britain not only eat more

In most developed countries, people can choose from thousands of different food products. In contrast, people in developing countries have few choices.

food than people in poorer countries but also are able to choose from a greater variety of foods. An average American shops in a supermarket that stocks literally thousands of different food products and enjoys a constantly varied diet. In comparison, even when well-fed, a peasant in a developing area of southeast Asia lives almost exclusively on rice and a handful of native vegetables.

The consequences of affluence

The developed countries can grow or buy all the food their peoples require and can provide widespread and inexpensive drinking water and electricity. They have extensive and well-maintained road systems, enabling people and goods to move swiftly from one place to another. The industrialized nations have access to advanced technology, so they produce large amounts of material goods and benefit from scientific research. Most citizens of developed countries are well-educated and employed. All these factors allow such nations to achieve high living standards for their growing populations.

As seen earlier, there is an important consequence of this prosperity. In order to maintain it, affluent countries must use vast amounts of the world's soil, water, fuels, and other resources. Population experts also recognize another consequence of enjoying high living standards. As people extract and use the earth's resources, they continuously alter the environment. This raises some serious questions, such as: How extensive are these environmental changes? Are the changes permanent? Are they harmful? Do people need to worry about them?

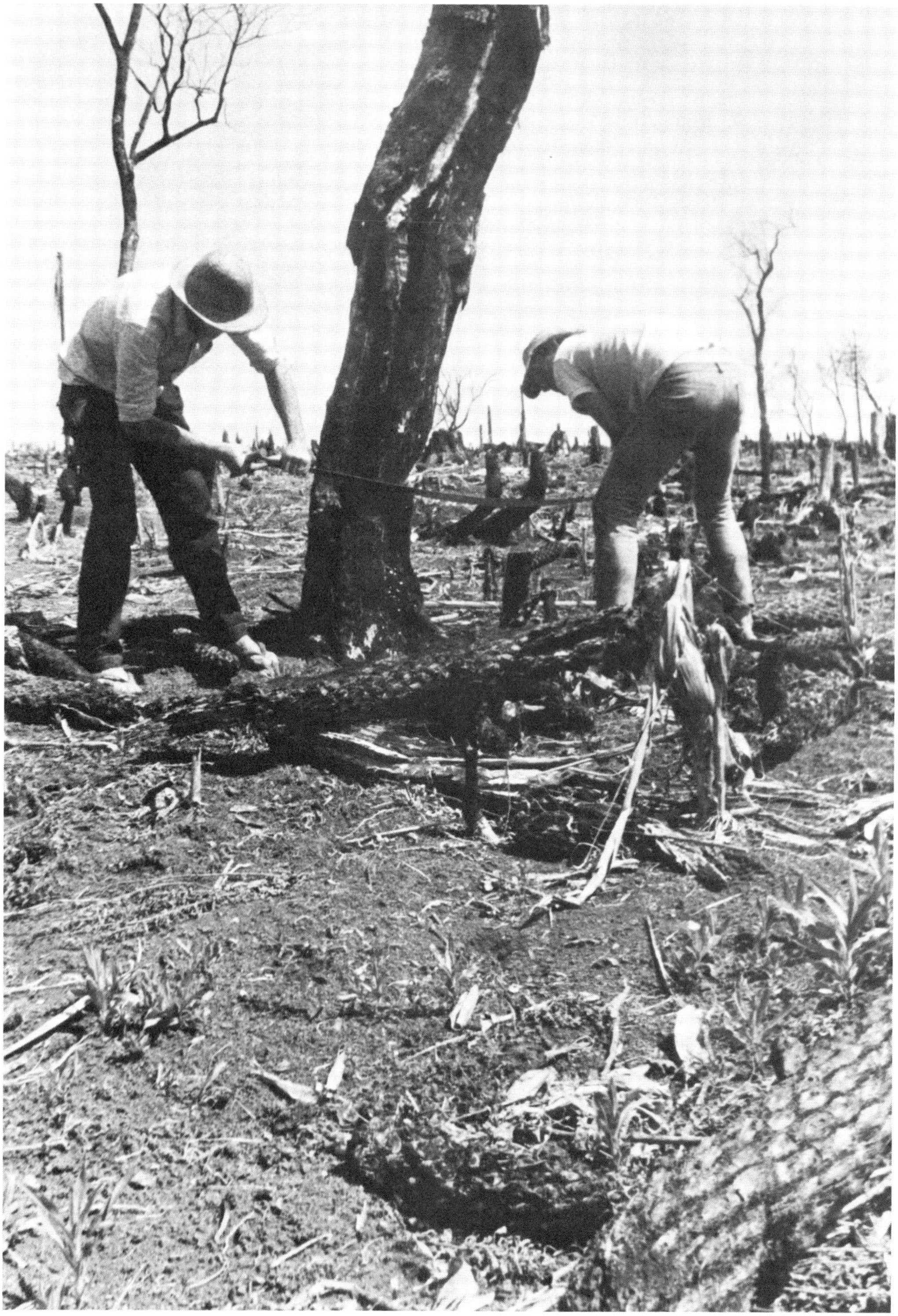

4

Dangers to the Environment

ONE OF THE MOST IMPORTANT population trends recognized by demographers, ecologists, and other scientists is the tendency for human populations to change the natural environment. People have always reshaped the environment to suit their own purposes. Expanding and migrating populations cleared forests for space to build homes and plant crops, as well as to get firewood and the timbers needed to construct ships. They dug canals for transportation and irrigation and dammed up rivers, creating new lakes. And they laid out thousands of miles of walls and fences, changing the habits and numbers of many migratory animals.

The impact of human demand

Usually, the larger a given population, the more it affects the environment. For example, more people require more food, so growing populations must devote more and more land to agriculture. To create new farmland, people must cut down more trees and divert more water for irrigation. These activities affect the environment and the creatures living within it in many different ways. Unfortunately, the effects are more often destruc-

(opposite page) In the Amazon rain forest, two farmers cut down a tree that remained after the entire area was burned to create space for food plantation. Experts are worried that people are destroying the environment to sustain an ever-increasing population.

tive than constructive. All over the world, in both developed and developing nations, human communities have polluted lakes, oceans, and the atmosphere; burned down precious forests; turned fertile land into desert; and driven species into extinction.

Sometimes the amount of environmental damage does not correspond to the number of people in a local population but rather to the wealth of those people. For one thing, rich countries that are not overpopulated often cause more pollution than poor nations with far larger populations.

Consider the ways that the exhaust from motor vehicles in the United States and China contribute to air pollution. In 1990, the United States had about 250 million people, while China had more than 1.1 billion people, more than four times as many. Yet experts estimate that exhaust from Chi-

In Ethiopia, deforestation is partly responsible for turning the once-fertile land to desert.

nese vehicles caused far less air pollution than emissions from American cars and trucks. Because the United States is a wealthier country with a higher standard of living, more Americans can afford to own cars. More cars mean more exhaust and, therefore, more air pollution.

Similarly, the average American buys and uses far more packaged material goods than an average Chinese. Many of these goods and virtually all of the packaging eventually get thrown away. Americans, though fewer in number than the Chinese, produce a great deal more garbage and litter.

This does not mean that it is better to live in China than in the United States. For one thing, China generates pollution in other ways. For instance, it allows many factories to discharge unfiltered smoke. And the United States continues to maintain much higher living standards than China, making it a much more comfortable place to live. Nevertheless, the fact remains that people in affluent countries tend to produce more environmental pollution per person than people in poor, overpopulated countries.

The density factor

Population density is another factor that affects the environment. When many people are concentrated in a small area, they may put an unusually heavy strain on the natural features of that area, sometimes completely reshaping it. The most obvious examples are densely populated cities where wood, concrete, metal, and tar have almost completely transformed natural environments into artificial ones. In the poorest of these cities— Mexico City and Calcutta for example—trees and other vegetation have been eliminated. Air and water pollution add to the environmental destruction in these areas.

Many experts, however, emphasize that popula-

Slums in Mexico City have sprouted up where natural vegetation once lived.

In Brazil, air pollution, soil erosion, and animal species extinctions result from the massive destruction of the forest.

tion density itself does not necessarily cause such destruction. Instead, overcrowding appears to worsen environmental damage only when the people involved are unable or unwilling to stop such damage. Comparing the Netherlands with Brazil illustrates this point. In 1990, the Netherlands had a high average population density of eleven hundred people per square mile yet boasted an excellent overall environmental record.

The Dutch government has waged a widespread campaign against air and water pollution. The people recycle most of their garbage, plant new trees, and practice soil and water conservation.

By contrast, Brazil's average population density was a relatively low forty-five people per square mile. Yet, according to the United Nations, Brazil has a poor environmental record. The Brazilians are cutting down their rain forests faster than ever before. This is part of the ongoing attempt to create homesteads and farmland for Brazil's growing population of poor and underprivileged people. Massive destruction of these forests contributes to air pollution and causes severe deforestation problems such as soil erosion and animal species extinctions. In addition, the Brazilian government continues to promote the massive building of roads and dams with little thought to resource conservation.

How people change the earth's surface

And so, population size, the degree of poverty or affluence of the people, and local population densities are all factors in environmental destruction. Yet these things do not cause the problem. It is people and their governments that cause such destruction when they fail to plan for their growing numbers, conserve natural resources, and control pollution.

Increasing human populations are transforming larger and larger tracts of the earth's surface for

The Itaipu dam in Brazil floods hundreds of miles of forest and farmland to supply water to a hydroelectric power plant.

Largest Urban Areas in the World in 1950, 1990 and 2000

○ 4 million and over since 1950
● 4 million and over since 1990
◉ 4 million and over in 2000 (projected)

Source: United Nations.

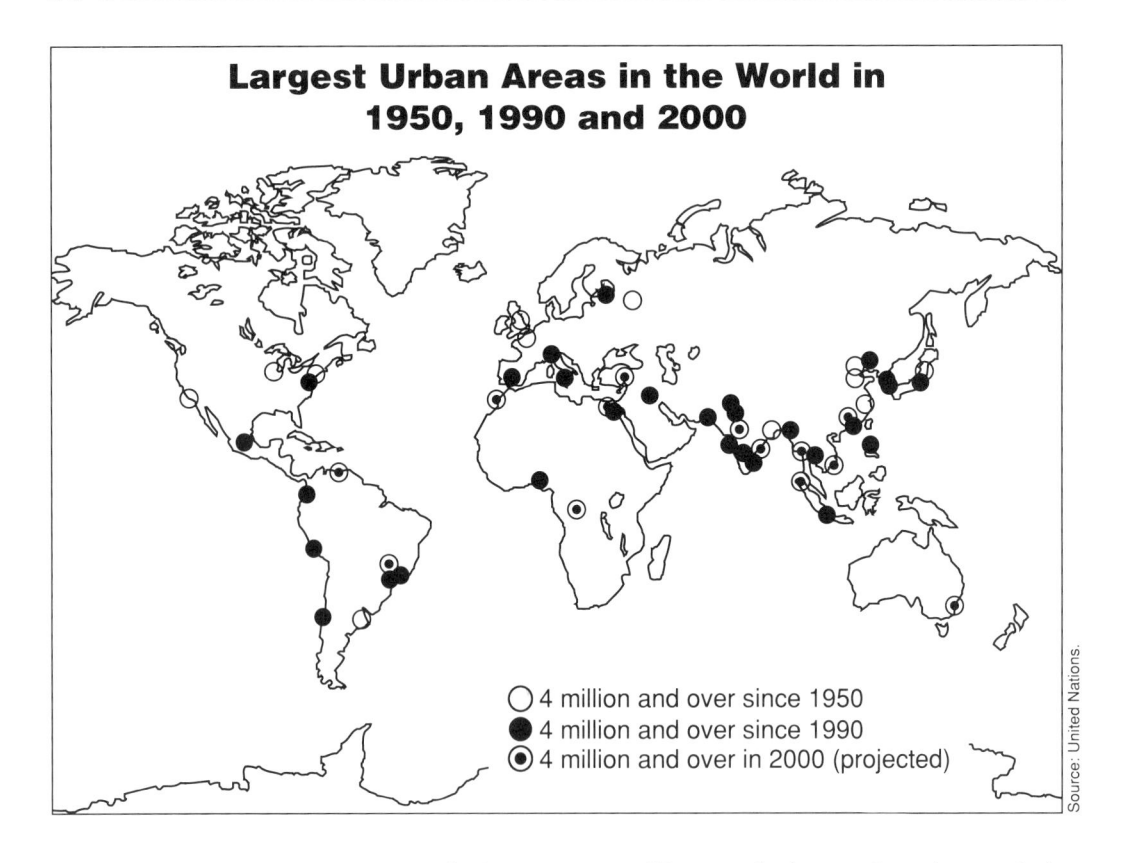

their own use. Human beings already exploit nearly all of the world's usable land. Usually, the land is developed without long-range planning. There is often little thought given to practicing resource conservation or curbing pollution. And rarely is the used land restored to its original state.

Consider how in the year 1990 people utilized different portions of the earth's land surfaces. About 11 percent was used to grow crops. Pastures for cows, goats, and other livestock accounted for another 25 percent. In many places, people have used the land year after year, without rotating crops or practicing other methods that help restore soil nutrients. As these areas produce less and less and finally wear out, people move on and create new farmland. Much of the old land remains unproductive and useless for many years.

Approximately 3 percent of the planet's land surface is paved over by cities, towns, and roads. This portion seems relatively small, but it encompasses 1.8 million square miles, or more than half the area occupied by the continental United States. And this portion of paved land continues to grow at a rate of thousands of square miles per year. With rare exceptions, people have permanently eliminated the natural environment from these areas, and they can no longer be used for growing food or harboring wildlife.

About 30 percent of the earth's land surface is still forested. According to biologists and other scientists, that is about half the amount that was forested before human beings began cutting down trees. People presently use large sections of the existing forests for activities ranging from lumbering to recreation. Some of the trees used are re-

Rubble and decay are all that remain in this abandoned New York City ghetto.

placed, but most are not. So as local populations increase, the percentage of forested land continues to shrink.

The remaining 31 percent of earth's land surface is covered by lakes and rivers or terrain of little or no use to people, such as mountaintops, deserts, and arctic ice packs. Since these areas cannot support human numbers of any consequence, they are not "available" for use by rapidly growing populations.

Human beings already use or abuse most of the world's available land. No vast new tracts of territory exist for expanding populations to exploit. This does not mean that the earth cannot support an even larger population. Because people do not always use the land in an efficient, economical manner, much of its potential is wasted. Better planning and resource conservation could allow the land already in use to support more people. Unfortunately, poor land use remains widespread, and abuse of the earth's environment continues.

Environmental problems in India

This relationship between increasing human populations and continued misuse of the environment is clearly illustrated in India. There, the problems of land and water use are extremely serious. With a population in 1990 of 835 million people, more than three times that of the United States, India must produce a great deal of food. Not surprisingly, virtually all of the unforested land is presently used for agriculture. There is considerable demand from Indian farmers and businesspeople to cut down the country's few remaining forests. This would not only create new farmland but also supply firewood and lumber for the nation's relentlessly growing population. But large-scale deforestation can badly damage the environment.

In the 1970s and 1980s, the Indian government publicly recognized the dangers of deforestation. It imposed limits on the number of acres that could be deforested each year. It also began programs to educate farmers, explaining that continued destruction of India's forests would eliminate precious water stores held in place by forest root systems. This would deplete the groundwater and make deforested areas harder to irrigate and difficult to replant. If India's forests disappear, it is unlikely that people will be able to replace them.

Black market lumber

The efforts of the Indian government to control deforestation have had mixed results. The rate of destruction of the valuable woodlands in the foothills of the Himalayan Mountains did slow somewhat in the 1980s. Still, demand for wood by the Indian population is so great that many people illegally harvest it. Thousands of black market Indian "owl men" regularly sneak out at night and cut down trees. Many Indians are seriously worried about the environmental damage caused by the owl men. Some of the most concerned citizens belong to the Chipko, or "tree hugger," movement. These men and women travel

In Brazil, thousands of acres of rain forest are burned to create farmland.

from village to village, educating people about the environmental importance of trees. Often, the tree huggers go out at night and use their own bodies to shield the trees from the axes of the owl men.

Another incident of destructive deforestation by an expanding human population occurred in Greece in ancient times. Greece had many forests and much fertile soil. As the Greek population grew, people cut down the forests for fuel and building materials and to create grazing land for goats and other animals. Most of the soil in the newly cleared areas eventually became depleted of nutrients because of overgrazing by animals. So people continued to cut down more trees and make more pastures. Almost no one considered what disastrous effects these activities might have on the environment. A few of the Greek philosophers warned that people should learn to plan better and conserve natural resources. But most people ignored these warnings. Today, Greece is almost totally without forests. Most of its soil is thin and only moderately fertile.

Rain forest destruction

Population pressures cause other serious deforestation problems. For instance, in Brazil, thousands of people are migrating from the overcrowded cities into the countryside in search of farmland. To clear new lands, these homesteaders currently burn down the country's vast rain forests at the rate of hundreds of acres per hour. This practice eliminates many thousands of plant and animal species that grow only in the forests. Biologists and ecologists worry that many little-known grains and other plants with potential to be future foodstuffs will be lost forever. They also fear the loss of many rare herbs and roots that might later be developed into drugs to fight such diseases as AIDS and cancer. Many experts say that the Brazilians are enjoying the short-term benefits of clearing the forests with little regard for the consequences.

A classic incident of environmental disaster brought on by the failure of a local population to plan ahead occurred in the Soviet Union in the 1950s. At the time, the Soviets began irrigating farmland surrounding the Aral Sea, then the fourth-largest natural lake in the world. Their plan was to greatly increase the food-producing capacity of the region in order to help feed its rapidly growing population.

The price of not planning ahead

The Soviets diverted water from rivers that fed the sea, assuming that the impact on the sea itself would be minimal. But they were wrong. By

Virtually all of the unforested land in India is used for agriculture, in an attempt to meet the needs of a growing population.

1989, the Aral had shrunk in area from over 25,600 square miles to about 16,000 square miles and had lost nearly two-thirds of its volume. Towns that used to be located on the shoreline are now many miles inland. The sea's once-rich fishing industry has almost completely disappeared.

In addition, Soviet planners failed to consider the buildup in the soil of salts and minerals from the diverted rivers. Much of the surrounding farmland is now a vast and useless salt bed more than two hundred miles across. A Soviet scientist traveling in the area described it as "what appeared to be a snow-covered plain stretching to the horizon without a sign of life." The project began as a way to meet the agricultural needs of an expanding population. The end result is a population that cannot adequately sustain itself and must import much of its food from other areas of the country.

Increasing levels of pollution

Another way expanding populations can harm the environment is by creating enormous amounts of waste and pollution. Increasing populations, especially in developed countries, create more demand for energy and material products. To meet these demands, power plants and factories must increase their output and, in the process, their production of wastes. Once again, poor planning and a disregard for environmental consequences come into play. Every day, large industries simply discharge huge amounts of these wastes into the air, waterways, and soil. For example, the Environmental Protection Agency (EPA) estimates that the U.S. chemical industry alone dumps sixty-eight billion pounds of toxic chemicals directly into American surface waters every year.

Sometimes, such actions are illegal. But the strictness of antipollution laws varies widely from country to country. For example, some nations allow factories to dump liquid wastes in rivers while others do not. Another problem is illegal dumping. Some companies secretly discharge their wastes under the cover of darkness. A few do so in broad daylight and routinely pay large fines for polluting. They figure that the cost of the fines is less than that of converting to new waste-disposal methods. Often, these companies knowingly pollute under the mistaken notion that nature can easily withstand the abuse.

Growing populations are also linked to increasing levels of air pollution. When a local population increases, people burn more wood and coal, refine more metals, and produce more wastes and hazardous chemicals. All of these activities contribute to air pollution. More people use more cars and other motor vehicles, the exhaust from which is the single largest contributor to air pollution.

Population density and distribution also affect the seriousness of air pollution. When a great

Growing populations are linked to increasing levels of pollution. Here, smog obscures visibility in downtown Los Angeles.

many people live and work in a relatively small area, as in a large city, their wastes and pollution become more concentrated in that area. And the wind often carries urban air pollutants to more distant areas, which then also suffer environmental damage.

When rainwater becomes toxic

A significant example of pollution created by crowded human populations is acid rain. Acid rain is composed of water droplets that contain high levels of sulfuric or nitric acid. Acid rain forms when airborne chemicals from power plants and factories react with water molecules in the air. Levels of acid rain have greatly increased in the 1970s and 1980s. This is because emissions from cars, factories, and power plants in or near heavily populated cities have increased. The more the population grows, the more the demand for cars. To produce the cars, more power plants must be built.

Acid rain is extremely harmful to the environment. When it falls into ponds and lakes, it increases the acidity of the water, which kills algae, fish and other organisms. A 1988 environmental study estimated that acid rain had made 25 percent of the lakes in New York's Adirondack Mountains incapable of supporting life. Acid rain also damages the leaves of trees and food crops. Germany's famous Black Forest suffered extensive acid rain damage in the 1970s and 1980s. In addition, acid rain eats away at marble, stone, and bronze. Many historic tombstones in Pennsylvania's Gettysburg National Military Park have become unreadable. And such classic monuments as the U.S. Capitol building and the temples on the Acropolis in Athens, Greece, are steadily eroding.

Many historic monuments have suffered extensive acid rain damage. The Acropolis in Greece, pictured here, is one example.

The Florida pattern

The relationship between population growth and environmental destruction was described in a well-known study completed in the mid-70s by ecologist Raymond F. Dasmann. He examined the expansion of Florida's population during the twentieth century and found that rampant, unplanned growth led to serious environmental problems. He called this the "Florida Pattern," a disturbing scenario that other studies have since confirmed. Many experts believe that any local population that grows too large too quickly is likely to roughly follow the Florida Pattern.

According to Dasmann's findings, in 1920 most of Florida was undeveloped wilderness, and the state had a population of about 1 million people. As time went on, the area's pleasant climate and recreational activities attracted more and more people. Unlike many areas of the world in which the population grows mainly because of high birthrates, Florida grew because of migration. By the early 1950s, there were 3 million people in the state. And by 1987, the population had risen to 12 million. This huge increase reflected a growth rate exceeding that of Bangladesh, one of the most overpopulated countries in the world. People continue to flock to Florida, and local officials expect the population to reach at least 17.5 million by the year 2010.

Uneven distribution

The problems associated with the Florida Pattern are not due simply to sheer numbers of people. Florida's population is also unevenly distributed. Drawn by beaches and the ocean, most people have settled in or near the large coastal urban centers like Miami and Palm Beach. One result is that years of overcrowding have caused serious erosion of the beaches in eastern Florida.

Adding to the crowding problem are the twenty-five million tourists a year who also go mostly to these cities. To accommodate all the visitors, extra houses, motels, stores, roads, boat yards, and other

In Florida, experts fear that expanding communities are ruining the Everglades and harming the wildlife, such as this young alligator.

facilities have to be built. By 1990, most of the east coast of the state had become a nearly continuous "strip city," an area where many small towns merge into one, long, developed "strip."

Destroying nature's handiwork

All the building and other human activity in eastern Florida devastated many local ecosystems. An ecosystem is a specific natural community that includes all the living creatures that inhabit the area as well as the environmental conditions, such as climate and landscape, that affect it. For instance, marshes, sandy beaches, and forest floors each contain their own unique ecosystems with specific plant and animal species. With little or no thought to the area's fragile network of ecosystems, developers in Florida cleared forests, filled in swamps, and destroyed marshes and other wetlands.

As a result of this massive development, many of the state's animal species are now endangered. These include the Florida manatee, a large water mammal thought to be the inspiration for mermaid legends, and the Florida beach mouse. Also headed for extinction are the key deer and the Florida panther, of which only thirty to fifty are left.

The interior sections of the state have also suffered. Developers sold tens of thousands of lots that lacked provisions for proper sewage. This led to problems in the disposal of human wastes. Many of these expanding communities are now encroaching on the Everglades and Big Cypress Park. The vast Everglades marshes are home for millions of fish, birds, and other animals and are a source of much of southern Florida's fresh water. People have already drained much of this water to support development and agriculture, disrupting the wildlife in the marsh ecosystems. For instance, ecologists estimate that only 10 percent of the original bird populations still live in the Everglades.

Lake Okeechobee, in the south-central portion of the state, another major source of fresh water, is heavily polluted. Demand for water by the human

Each year, twenty-five million tourists flock to the beaches of Florida, compounding the crowding problems.

population of the area is so great that underground water tables surrounding the lake have noticeably dropped in the last decade.

An example to others

All of these factors of the Florida Pattern—overcrowding, overdevelopment, water pollution, and destruction of ecosystems—threaten to destroy Florida's natural environment. Florida officials are aware of these problems and have taken some steps toward eliminating them. These steps include stricter rules governing development and tougher penalties for illegal polluters. Whether or not these and other efforts will be successful remains to be seen.

Population experts hope that the situation in Florida will serve as an example to people elsewhere. It dramatically illustrates what can happen when rapid population growth is accompanied by a lack of forethought and a disregard for nature's delicate balance. The scientists hope that people in other areas of the world will try to avoid the Florida Pattern. This can be done by finding better ways to manage land and water, control pollution, and discourage overcrowding. And the key to making it all work is planning ahead.

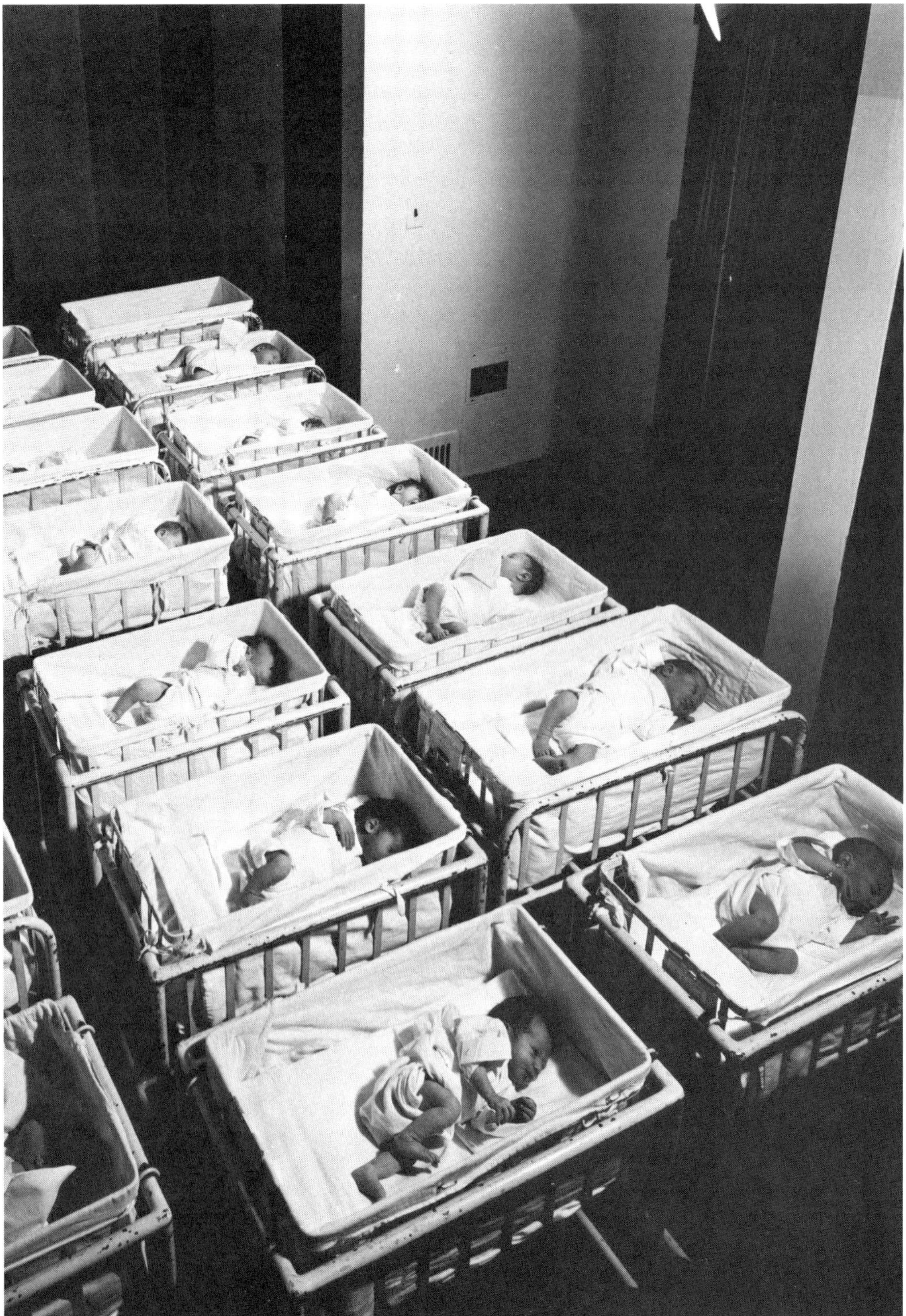

5
Population Strategies and Solutions

WITH SCIENTISTS PREDICTING that the world's population will top ten billion during the next century, population growth has become one of the most important and controversial social issues. Private and government-sponsored researchers around the world try to recognize and predict population trends and problems. They also seek ways to plan for and solve these problems.

Differing approaches to the problems

The most significant population problems are those examined earlier in this book: poverty and overpopulation in poor, nonindustrialized countries, widespread hunger and malnutrition, disease and unsanitary living conditions, destruction of the environment, and lack of environmental planning.

There is considerable disagreement among various experts and organizations about how to properly address these issues. Opinions break down into two major viewpoints. The first group sees most population-related problems as various aspects of one large underlying problem: too many people in the world. The principal approach of

(opposite page) An array of newborn babies rests in cribs in a New York hospital. Many experts believe that population-related problems can be solved by lowering the birthrate.

Increasing worldwide demand for energy has prompted the development of alternative energy sources, such as this experimental solar energy collector in New Mexico.

those who hold this view is to encourage people to have fewer children.

The other group of people contends that there are not too many people in the world. Those expressing this opinion believe that poverty, malnutrition, and starvation are caused by an uneven distribution of people, money, and resources. This group wants to develop new and better technologies for growing food and producing energy, rather than discourage people from having children.

Room for unlimited growth

The "new development" strategy proposes that the world's food and other resources are unlimited. According to this view, it is only people's knowledge of how to produce and use these resources that is limited. Therefore, as people acquire new knowledge, they find better ways to support their populations. Economist Jacqueline Kasun says:

> The types and quantities of economic resources are continually changing, as is the ability of given areas to support life. In the same territories in which earlier men struggled and starved, much larger populations today support themselves in comfort. The difference, of course, lies in the *knowledge* that human beings bring to the task of discovering and managing resources.

The key resource is the human imagination, according to Kasun and others, including economist Julian Simon. According to this view, if a certain resource appears to be running out, one of two things will happen. The first possibility is that people will discover new ways to find and extract more of that resource. For example, coal production might become limited by the depth at which coal miners can work. People will then invent new mining technologies that allow the miners to dig deeper. The other possibility is that people will find an adequate substitute for the resource. For instance, if there is a scarcity of iron, people could use aluminum as a substitute. Or, if oil runs out, an alternative energy source could replace it.

But, Simon points out, people will not resort to these actions unless there is sufficient demand for them to do so. Many forms of energy and raw materials appear limited because the demand to increase or replace them is not yet great enough. So people presently do not spend the time nor do the research necessary to discover the alternatives. For example, there are only so many coal deposits in the ground and people will eventually run out of coal. Yet, existing coal supplies are enough to last humanity another two hundred years. That is a

An Asian street vendor sells American-made canned goods. The importing and exporting of commodities from one country to another may help alleviate the uneven distribution of food throughout the world.

long time, so no one is particularly worried about running out of coal and there is no pressing demand to find a replacement for it.

What will create the demand to increase or replace the world's resources and thereby stimulate the necessary research? More population growth will create this demand, according to Kasun, Simon, and others. "The more people, the more minds there are to discover new deposits and increase productivity, with raw materials as with other goods," Simon says. He explains that as long as there is population growth, energy and resources are unlimited. This view maintains that the more people there are, the more the need arises for energy and resources to sustain them. And, as it becomes necessary, people will expand their horizons and search for these resources. Simon concludes:

> Now we have begun to explore the sea, which contains amounts of metallic and other resources that dwarf any deposits we know about on land. And we have begun to explore the moon. Why shouldn't the boundaries of the system from which we derive resources continue to expand in such directions, just as they have expanded in the past? This is one more reason not to regard resources as "finite."

Food for the multitudes

But will there be enough food to feed all the new people who will create the demand for new resources? Demographer Colin Clark, former director of the Agricultural Economic Institute at Oxford University, believes there will be enough food. He studied present world food production and concluded that improved farming methods could grow enough food to feed 35 billion people a year on an American-type diet. Since this diet is much richer than is necessary to sustain life, Clark estimated that the world could actually sustain up to 105 billion people, more than twenty times its present population.

Roger Revelle, former director of the Harvard Center for Population Studies, agrees. He estimates that the world's existing agricultural resources could supply enough cloth, rubber, and beverages for at least forty billion people. Like Simon, Revelle sees no limit to potential future production. He blames current population problems on poor social attitudes and government policies. He emphasizes, "The world's food problem does not arise from any physical limitation on potential output or any danger of unduly stressing the environment. The limitations on abundance are to be found in the social and political structures of nations and in the economic relations among them."

Attempts to redistribute food

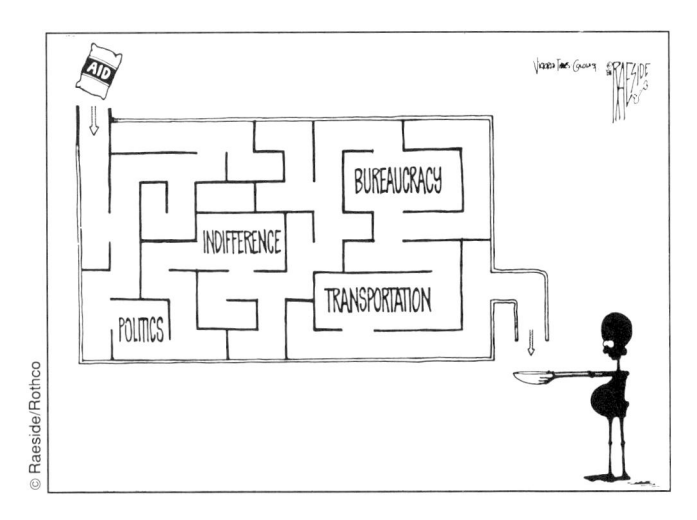

To correct the uneven distribution of food, the rich countries with more food than they need have tried shipping excess food to the poor, needy countries. Those who advocate such food aid argue that the United States, Canada, and other major food producers accumulate huge food surpluses each year. They insist that this extra food can help end world hunger. In fact, the United States and other countries do periodically make such large-scale donations of foodstuffs.

Difficulties in distribution

Unfortunately, these charitable endeavors are usually not completely successful. This is because getting the food to the hungry is often difficult and sometimes even impossible. For example, during the 1980s, the United States and other wealthy nations sent a great deal of food to help relieve the famine in central Africa. But much of the food never reached the hungry. As mentioned earlier, this was partly because of local violence and a shortage of roads and trucks.

Another reason these relief efforts were largely ineffective was the difficulty of transporting the amount of food needed fast enough. Large transport planes can carry only about 20 tons of material in a single trip. In Africa, the hungry needed at least 1.5 million tons of grain per year, which means that about seventy-five thousand plane trips would have been required. The time needed to complete so many trips, as well as the cost of fuel for the planes, made such a massive airlift impossible.

Ships are also used to transport food. But port facilities can handle only a certain number of ships at a time. Experts estimate that it would have taken at least two years to unload 1.5 million tons of grain in African ports. During that time, the region's population increased by another three million people. So even if all the grain had gotten through, there still would not have been enough to feed everyone.

Clearly, although food donations from rich to poor nations are helpful and always appreciated, they are not the ultimate solution to ending world hunger.

A child waits for food at a Sudanese refugee camp.

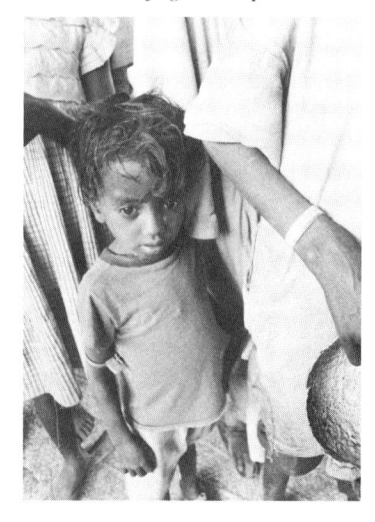

Another approach to feeding hungry populations is the invention of new and more productive farming techniques. "New development" advocates such as Simon and Revelle believe that this approach will enable all countries to feed much larger populations in the future. They point out that new farming technology has helped feed hundreds of millions of people in the second half of the twentieth century.

A convoy of food arrives in Ethiopia. Transporting excess food to needy countries is difficult and often ineffective.

A food-growing revolution

After World War II, scientists learned to breed special varieties of major crops like wheat, corn, and rice. When planted with new types of fertilizers, these crops became "high yield," producing many more plants per acre. This so-called "Green Revolution" resulted in a threefold increase in the world's food output between 1945 and 1990. Most of the Green Revolution's successes oc-

To feed hungry populations, scientists have developed special varieties of crops like rice, wheat, and corn. Here, Vietnamese farmers harvest a specially developed strain of rice that is high yielding and resistant to pests.

curred in already productive countries like the United States, Canada, and Australia. Some less-developed nations, notably Mexico, India, and China, also benefited greatly from the new techniques. Between 1950 and 1980, Mexico's grain production increased fourfold.

One important aspect of the Green Revolution is biotechnology, the transplanting of plant genes from one crop species to another. Genes are the microscopic material in all organisms that determine the characteristics of the organism. Scientists take genes from the healthiest, most successful plants and combine them with genes from other plants in order to make the weaker plants more productive.

Using such tricks of genetic engineering, researchers are attempting to produce new varieties of known plants. They hope these new crops will have a higher yield, need less water to grow, and be more resistant to insects and other pests. Some experts, among them economists Colin Clark and Peter Bauer, believe that continued successes in this area will eventually solve the world's hunger problems. According to this view, science will continue to provide the means to transform nonproductive land into productive land. Farmers who presently have no means or hope of growing more food will someday be able to do so. And countries like Mexico and India will continue to match population increases with higher crop yields.

Failing to keep up with demand

Other experts, notably biologist Paul Ehrlich and renowned demographer Kingsley Davis, disagree. They say the claims that the Green Revolution will solve the world's hunger problems have not been tested. They admit that biotechnology is promising and beneficial. But, they insist, it has limits and may not be able to keep up with the needs of the world's rapidly expanding population.

Ehrlich and Davis are two of the leading advocates of solving population problems by limiting the number of people. In sharp contrast to the optimistic "new development" strategy, the "limit reproduction" approach is based on the belief that there will *not* be enough food, energy, and resources to sustain ever-growing populations. Therefore, people should find some way to keep human numbers from getting any larger. Those who support this approach agree that the introduction of new and better technologies for food production will help relieve the problems of overpopulation. But, they say, the development of such technologies is already failing to keep pace with expanding populations.

Organizations such as the Planned Parenthood Federation and the Worldwatch Institute (both headquartered in Washington, D.C.) argue that governments are not adequately planning ahead. In particular, they say, there has not been enough new development of energy and resources. For instance, due to lack of government funding, research into alternative energy sources, such as solar, wind, and geothermal power, actually decreased in the 1980s. And during that time, no new nuclear plants were built or ordered in the United States, according to the Worldwatch Institute.

In addition, oil-producing countries found only a few new oil deposits and did not significantly advance oil-drilling technology in the 1980s. But demand for oil continued to increase, mostly by affluent, developed populations. In response to

Some experts believe that governments need to spend more money on the development of new energy sources, such as solar, wind, and geothermal power. Here, a line of windmills harnesses the power of the wind.

this demand, oil companies pumped more oil, but they did not markedly improve their ability to do so in the future.

The solution to these problems, according to economist Lester Brown, science writer Isaac Asimov, and many others, is to slow and finally stabilize the growth of the world's population. They argue that fewer people would demand less energy as well as fewer resources and material goods. With a relatively slow-growing population, resources would last longer. Also new scientific advances would then have more time to develop and would keep pace with new demands.

Population-control advocates suggest that limiting the number of people would bring other benefits. For one thing, there would be more food to go around. This would reduce hunger in poor countries. Able to feed themselves, inhabitants of rural areas would feel less pressured to migrate to cities searching for jobs, and cities would not grow as fast. Proponents of this view argue that in time, technical and economic improvements would make living conditions in both the cities and the countryside more tolerable. In addition, a smaller population would generate less pollution and create fewer environmental problems.

Controlling birthrates

The way to slow population growth is to control birthrates, according to the population-control approach. The late anthropologist Margaret Mead said, "Birth control is the only humane and rational answer to our population dilemma." Organizations like Planned Parenthood as well as population strategists like Steven Sinding of the U.S. Agency for International Development (AID) agree. They have as their goal the worldwide attainment of zero population growth (ZPG). This occurs when no more people are born than die, so

In Kenya, a doctor lectures villagers on devices that prevent pregnancy. Population-control advocates believe that effective family planning can reduce hunger and improve living conditions in poor countries.

the population remains the same.

The effort to limit human numbers has met with some success in many of the wealthy developed countries. For example, the United States, West Germany, and Denmark achieved a condition of near-ZPG in the 1970s. Japan, Canada, and the Soviet Union also brought their population growth rates as low as 0.5 to 0.7 percent per year. But these growth rates began to rise again in the late 1980s. In May 1990, the U.S. National Center for Health Statistics reported that the U.S. population growth rate had risen since it reached its all-time low in 1976. ZPG advocates hope this rate will decrease again in the near future.

In the meantime, population growth rates in most developing countries remain high. Planned Parenthood and the Worldwatch Institute as well as several United Nations agencies want to lower these rates. They believe that education is the best method for getting people to have fewer children. Representatives of these groups live in or travel to countries with rapidly growing populations. As a first step, the population workers inform people about the social and economic problems associated with having too many children. The workers then offer information about how to plan family size and how to obtain and use contraceptives, devices that prevent pregnancy. They also give advice on disease prevention and nutrition so that more children will survive. The workers hope that fewer children dying will be an incentive for couples to have smaller families.

Those who want to lower the rate of population growth say that their approach has worked in the past. Lester Brown says, "Countries that have made the shift to small families typically have four things in common: an active national population education program, widely available family planning services, incentives for small families . . . and widespread improvements in economic and social conditions."

A dramatic decrease in the rate of population growth occurred recently in China. In the early 1970s, Chinese leaders became worried about their country's population, which had already surpassed 900 million. They feared that as the population continued to grow, the nation would sink further into the poverty and famine that have

This graph illustrates the effects of different growth rates on a population. For example, a population of five million that grows at a rate of 4 percent will reach ten million in seventeen years.

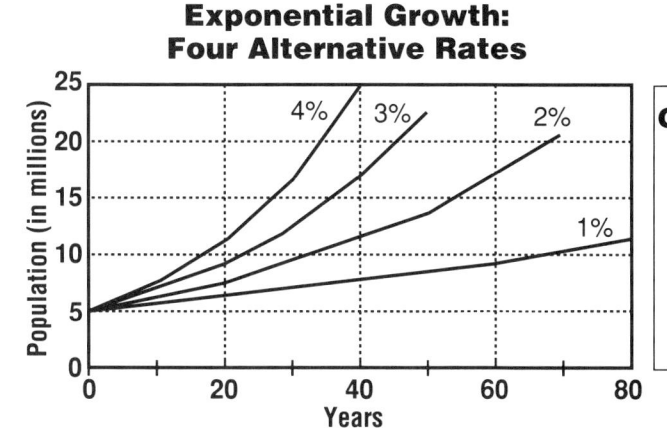

Exponential Growth: Four Alternative Rates

Growth Rate	Doubling Time
1%	70 years
2%	35 years
3%	23 years
4%	17 years

Source: United Nations Population Division.

plagued China for centuries. In 1974, China became the first country in history to adopt the official goal of not only stabilizing but also decreasing its population. The government's aim was to stabilize the number of people at 1.2 billion, then begin a slow but steady reduction to about 700 million people.

Success at a price

The Chinese population program achieved impressive results but at a decided cost in individual freedoms. The effort succeeded in lowering the population growth rate to about 1 percent by the mid-1980s. The Chinese achieved this mainly through implementing extensive education programs. The programs urged people to have only one and certainly no more than two offspring. But the government feared that too many people would ignore the advice and decide to stick with traditional ideas about having large families. So Chinese officials sometimes resorted to force. They encouraged people to publicly denounce couples who had more than two children. Some of these couples also received punishments such as job demotions and pay reductions. There are even rumors that authorities forced some women to have abortions, or end their pregnancies early. These rumors remain unconfirmed. "Limit reproduction" advocates are pleased with China's results but not necessarily with its methods. They hope that other countries will not choose to adopt such extreme measures.

The dilemma faced by more and more governments around the world is which approach to use in formulating a national population policy. Should they accept the "new development" strategy and emphasize inventing new ways to support ever-growing populations? Or should they adopt the "limit reproduction" approach and educate people to have fewer children? The advocates of each viewpoint are often openly critical of their opponents. The ZPG proponents accuse the others of talking nonsense and encouraging planetwide disaster. Those who advocate unlimited growth call their opponents "prophets of doom," saying their arguments are founded on faulty evidence. Each side has an impressive collection of data and seemingly logical predictions to back up its claims. As a result, it is very difficult for government leaders to come to a decision on this vitally important issue.

Erasing debts

Occasionally, advocates of both approaches agree. For instance, all of those concerned believe it is important to stimulate and strengthen the economies of poor developing nations. One suggested way of doing this is to convince the wealthy developed countries to forgive the debts owed to them by poorer countries. Proponents of

A 1982 billboard in China encourages the birth of only one child per family. Although China's program to decrease population proved effective, many think that it infringed upon individual freedoms.

this idea argue that a high proportion of the yearly budget of a developing nation must go to make debt payments. If these debts were erased, that money could be used to purchase advanced farming equipment or to educate people about having smaller families. Many people say that countries like the United States and Great Britain could afford to take such action.

Many government officials in developed countries, however, believe that forgiving Third World debts is not the answer to poverty and other population problems. They argue that such measures would bring only small and temporary improvements. Also, this would set a bad example, sending the signal to countries around the world that it is all right to borrow money and not pay it back. No one has tried erasing debts between countries on a large scale, so the idea remains untested.

It may be that, at present, no one knows how

In Bangladesh, couples listen to a government spokesperson talk about population goals.

best to deal with the population dilemma. Perhaps there is not yet enough data available for people to make the proper decisions about population-related issues. For the time being, scientists and government leaders can only continue to study the available information, draw conclusions, and make predictions based on those conclusions.

Looking toward the future

There is one other point that all those concerned about world population agree on. It is that people should treat population-related problems seriously and continue to search for workable solutions. Finding ways to end poverty, feed the hungry, house the homeless, and save the environment will surely benefit humanity in the future. If people eventually solve these problems, all members of future generations will enjoy a better quality of life.

Isaac Asimov says, "If the crisis [of overpopulation] is beaten . . . we may have a world population that is declining toward some permanent safe level. We may also have a world without war, and one that is used to working together. We may have a world that is uniformly prosperous and not one that is divided into rich and poor nations." Then, he says, "humanity can truly reach out beyond the Earth to other worlds, and become more powerful and happy than we can imagine today."

Glossary

acid rain: Atmospheric water droplets containing high levels of sulfuric or nitric acid.

biotechnology: The transplanting of genes from one plant species to another in order to improve the various qualities of the plants.

carrying capacity: The population that an area can adequately sustain given the available resources.

contraceptive: A device that prevents pregnancy.

demographer: A person who studies population statistics, trends, patterns, and problems.

developed countries: Industrialized nations, usually having overall high living standards.

developing countries: Non- or semi-industrialized nations, usually having generally poor living standards.

infant mortality: The deaths of babies and young children.

malnutrition: The lack of a proper diet.

overpopulation: A condition in which a given population does not have the amount of food and other resources it needs to sustain itself.

population checks: Factors that work to slow population growth. Positive checks include disease, famine, and war. Preventive checks are efforts made by people to limit their own numbers.

population density: The measure of the number of people living within a given unit of area, for instance, 250 people per square mile.

population distribution: The way people form patterns by living either close together or far apart.

population growth rate: A measurement of how fast a given population expands.

Third World: General term describing non- and semi-industrialized countries with poor living standards.

zero population growth (ZPG): A condition in which a population's birthrate and death rate are about equal and the number of people remains stable.

Suggestions for Further Reading

Isaac Asimov, *Earth: Our Crowded Spaceship*. Greenwich, CT: Fawcett Publications, 1974.

P.A.A. Berle, "Five Billion and Counting," *Audubon*, July 1987

David Berreby, "The Numbers Game," *Discover*, April 1990.

Paul R. Ehrlich and Anne H. Ehrlich, "Population, Plenty and Poverty," *National Geographic*, December 1988.

Eric McGraw, *Population Growth*. Vero Beach, FL: Rourke Enterprises, 1987.

L. Oliwenstein, "Billions and Billions and Billions," *Discover*, January 1988.

Works Consulted

Lester R. Brown, Christopher Flavin, and Sandra Postel, *State of the World 1989*. New York: W.W. Norton, 1989.

Colin Clark, *The Myth of Overpopulation*. Houston: Lumen Christi, 1975.

Paul R. Ehrilch and Anne H. Ehrlich, *The Population Explosion*. New York: Simon & Schuster, 1990.

R.S. Fosler, "Demographics of the 90s," *Vital Speeches of the Day*, July 1, 1989.

Frances Frech, *Out of Africa: Some Population Truths*. Kansas City, MO: Population Renewal Office, 1988.

Pranay Gupte, *The Crowded Earth: People and the Politics of Population*. New York: W.W. Norton, 1984.

G.J. Hardin, "How Many Creatures?" *Bioscience*, April 1987.

Jacqueline Kasun, *The War Against Population*. San Francisco: Ignatius Press, 1988.

N. Keyfitz, "The Growing Human Population," *Scientific American*, September 1989.

R. Cort Kirkwood, "The Population Bomb. . . Defused," *The Freeman*, November 1989.

Thomas B. Littlewood, *The Politics of Population*. Notre Dame, IN: University of Notre Dame Press, 1979.

James L. Newman and Gordon E. Matzke, *Population: Patterns, Dynamics and Prospects*. Englewood Cliffs, NJ: Prentice-Hall, 1984.

Ray Percival, "Malthus and His Ghost," *National Review*, August 18, 1989.

Julian L. Simon, *The Ultimate Resource*. Princeton, NJ: Princeton University Press, 1981.

UN Chronicle, "Population Pressures Contributing to Environmental Damage," September 1988.

B.J. Wattenberg, "Lower Birthrates Spell a Brighter Future for the Third World," *U.S. News & World Report*, December 18, 1989.

L. Williamson, "The Ultimate Wildlife Threat," *Outdoor Life*, December 1987.

Index

acid rain, 64-65
Africa, 12-13
  famine in, 9, 15, 16, 76
air pollution, 52-53, 54-55, 63-64
Aral Sea, 61-62
Asimov, Isaac, 81, 87
Australia, 21, 77-78

Bangladesh, 15, 24
  overpopulation in, 66
Bauer, Peter, 78-79
biotechnology, 78, 79
birth control, 81, 83
Black Forest, 65
Bombay, India, 26, 27-29
Brazil, 25
  forest destruction in, 54-55, 60-61
Brown, Lester, 81, 83

Canada
  population growth in, 82
  wealth of, 12, 21, 77-78
chawls, 28
children, 37
  malnutrition and starvation of, 15, 32-34
  population control and, 71-72, 82-83, 84
China, 78
  air pollution in, 52-53
  famine in, 7-9, 35-36
  population control in, 83-84
cities
  environmental destruction and, 53, 57
  overcrowding in, 26-27, 30-31
  poverty in, 25, 81
Clark, Colin, 74-75, 78-79
coal supplies, 72-74
Colombia, poverty in, 16-18, 24

Dasmann, Raymond F., 65-66

Davis, Kingsley, 79
deforestation, 54-55, 57-58, 59-61
demographers, 12, 13, 51
Denmark, population growth, 82
developed countries
  food production and consumption, 46-49
  industry and technology, 18-21, 39-41
  living standards in, 41-42
  population in, 12, 46
  resource consumption, 42-43, 49
  Third World debt and, 85-87
  wealth from trade, 43-46
developing countries
  food distribution problems in, 34-37
  foreign debt of, 23, 85-87
  malnutrition and starvation in, 15-16, 31-34
  natural resources of, 23, 42
  overcrowding in, 26-27, 28-30, 31
  population growth in, 18-21, 82-83
  poverty in, 12-15, 23, 25-26, 30-31, 40
  wealthy in, 23-24, 27-28
diseases, 7, 15-16, 71
  population control and, 34
  prevention of, 60, 83
drought, 7

education, 41
Ehrlich, Paul, 79
electricity
  developed countries and, 41-42, 49
  developing countries and, 26, 30, 31
endangered species, 67-68
energy consumption, 42-43, 79-80
environmental destruction, 87
  deforestation, 54-55, 57-58, 59-61
  farming and, 51-52, 59, 61-62, 75
  Florida pattern, 65-69

land use and, 55-59
pollution, 52-53, 62-65
population density and, 53-54, 81
Environmental Protection Agency (EPA), 62
Ethiopia
  famine in, 9, 36-37
  poverty in, 15, 18, 19, 24

famine
  Africa and, 15, 16, 76
  China and, 7-9, 35-36
  Ethiopia and, 9, 36-37
  population control and, 34
farming, 37
  crop failure and, 7
  developing countries and, 18, 56
  environmental destruction and, 51-52, 59, 61-62
  industrialized, 40, 46-47
  population growth and, 74, 75, 76-77, 79
Florida, 66-69
food
  developed countries and, 47-49
  developing countries and, 7, 15-16, 32, 59
  distribution problems, 34-37, 75-76
  population growth and, 34-35, 81
  production improvements, 74-75, 77-78
foreign debt, 23, 85-87
forests, 57-58, 59
  Brazil, 54-55, 60-61

Germany, 65
  population growth in, 82
Gettysburg National Military Park, 65
governments, population control, 79-80, 84
Greece, 60, 65
Green Revolution, 77-78, 79
Gupte, Pranay, 25-27

Haiti, 24
Hartley, Shirley, 21
hepatitis, 30
homelessness, 25, 31, 39
housing shortages, 27-28, 31

income
  developed countries and, 19, 41
  developing countries and, 14, 18, 41
India, 78, 79
  cholera epidemic in, 15
  environmental destruction in, 58-60
  food costs in, 48
  overcrowding in, 25-26, 27-30, 31
  per capita income, 41
  poverty in, 24, 25
industry
  developed countries and, 39, 40
  developing countries and, 24-25
  environmental pollution, 53, 62-63, 64
infant mortality, 15, 33
irrigation, 51, 61-62

Japan
  population growth of, 82
  wealth of, 18-19, 43

Kasun, Jacqueline, 72, 74

lakes and rivers, 58
land use, 55-58
living standards
  developed countries and, 12, 19, 21, 41-42, 48, 49
  developing countries and, 15-16, 23, 25, 71, 81

malnutrition, 7, 15, 31-34, 71, 72
Malthus, Thomas Robert, 34
manufactured goods, 40
Mexico, 25, 78, 79
Mexico City, 29-30, 31, 53
Moraes, Dom, 16-18

natural resources
  developed countries and, 12, 20, 21, 39-40, 42-44, 49
  developing countries and, 23, 42
  population growth and, 72-73, 74
Ndong, F. Nguema, 33-34
Netherlands, 45-46, 54
New Zealand, 19-21
Nicaragua
  per capita income, 41
  poverty in, 19-21, 24

oil, 44-45, 80-81

overpopulation, 7, 71-72, 87
  China and, 9
  developing countries and, 13, 23, 30
  Florida and, 66
  India and, 25-26
  Nicaragua and, 20

Pakistan, 24
Peru, 24
Planned Parenthood Federation, 79, 82
pollution, 52-53, 54
  acid rain, 64-65
  Florida and, 68
  population growth and, 62-64, 81
population density, 19, 26, 53-54
population growth, 18, 71, 74
  China and, 83-84
  environmental destruction and, 62-64, 65-66, 69, 81
  food shortages and, 34-35
  reducing, 81-83, 87
poverty
  developed countries and, 39
  developing countries and, 12-15, 24, 25, 30, 32, 37
  elimination of, 72, 86-87
  population growth and, 13-14, 18, 23, 33, 71, 72
Pyrelal, Shaila, 28-29, 30, 37

rainfall, 7-8, 9
Revelle, Roger, 75, 77

sanitation, 15, 26, 30, 41
Saudi Arabia, 43-45
semideveloped countries, 24-25
shantytowns, 28
Simon, Julian, 72-73, 74, 77
Soviet Union, 61-62, 82
starvation, 7, 9, 15, 31-34, 72
Struthers, Sally, 32-33
Sudan, 24, 43
  famine in, 9, 37

technology
  developed countries and, 19, 20, 21, 39, 47, 49
  developing countries and, 18, 20, 23
  elimination of poverty and, 72, 77, 79

Third World. *See* developing countries
Torres, Georgina de, 17-18, 21
trade, 19, 20
transportation, 31, 39, 49
  food distribution problems and, 35, 36, 76

Uganda, 24
United Nations, 32, 46, 82
United Nations Children's Fund, 15
United States
  Agency for International Development (AID), 81
  air pollution in, 52-53, 65
  Bureau of the Census, 12
  energy consumption of, 42-43, 80
  food relief, 76
  food spending in, 48
  National Center for Health Statistics, 82
  per capita income, 41
  population growth in, 82
  Population Reference Bureau, 11
  wealth of, 12, 21, 77-78

Vasquez, Hilda, 29-30
Vista Hermosa, Colombia, 16-17

war
  Ethiopia and, 36-37
  Nicaragua and, 20
  population control and, 34
water supplies
  contaminated, 15, 17
  developed countries and, 41, 46, 49
  developing countries and, 26, 30, 31, 59
  irrigation and, 51, 61-62
  pollution and, 62-63, 64-65, 68-69
wealthy, in poor countries, 23-24, 27-28
welfare programs, 41
World Bank, 14, 32, 42, 46
world population, 11-12, 24, 71, 74-75
World Resources Institute, 45
Worldwatch Institute, 79, 82

zero population growth, 81-82, 85

About the Author

Don Nardo is an actor, makeup arist, film director, composer, and teacher, as well as a writer. As an actor, he has appeared in more than fifty stage productions, including several Shakespeare plays. He has also worked before or behind the camera in twenty films. Several of his musical compositions, including a young person's version of H.G. Wells's *The War of the Worlds*, have been played by regional orchestras. Mr. Nardo's writing credits include short stories, articles, textbooks, screenplays, and several teleplays, including an episode of ABC's "Spenser: For Hire." In adddition, his screenplay *The Bet* won an award from the Massachusetts Artists Foundation. Mr. Nardo lives with his wife and son on Cape Cod, Massachusetts.

Picture Credits

Photos supplied by Research Plus, Inc., Mill Valley, California

Cover photo by Helena Frost Associates, LTD.
Air France, 38; AP/Wide World Photos, 30, 43, 60, 76; The Bettmann Archive, 34, 65, 70; John Deere, © Montes De Oca, 13 (right); 40; Helena Frost, FPG, 52; H.J. Heinz, 73; H.U.D., 57; The Pathfinder Fund, 53, 82, 86; Reuters/Bettmann, 17, 25, 28, 35, 50, 54, 80; UNICEF/981/85/Ethiopia, John Richardson, 22; UNICEF/987/85/Ethiopia, John Richardson, 24; United Nations, 10, 32; United Nations/Ray Cranbourne, 44; United Nations/J. Frank, 14; United Nations/John Isaac, 77, 85; United Nations/P. Levy, 31; United Nations/Derek Lovejoy, 72; United Nations/Kate Rader, 15; United Nations/ A. Rozberg, 13 (left); United Nations/P.S. Sudhakaran, 26; United Nations/Ray Witlin, 19; United Nations/B.P. Wolff, 18; United Nations Photo/UNICEF Photo, Magubane, 6; UPI/Bettmann, 8, 16, 20, 21, 27, 36, 42, 48, 55, 63, 67, 68, 78; USDA, 41; World Bank Photo/Ray Witlin, 1977, 61